MORTAL MATTERS

MORTAL

Sara Engram

MATTERS

When a Loved One Dies

Andrews and McMeel
A Universal Press Syndicate Company
Kansas City • New York

Library of Congress Cataloging-in-Publication Data

Engram, Sara.
  Mortal matters : when a loved one dies / Sara Engram.
    p.   cm.
  ISBN 0-8362-2623-2 : $7.95
  1. Death—Social aspects—United States. Funeral rites and customs—
United States—Planning. 3. Grief. I. Title.
HQ1073.5.U6E54   1990
306.9—dc20   90-30948
                                                     CIP

Designed by Rick Cusick.

Contents

Introduction

I'm going to die.

There. I've said it.

It wasn't easy. In fact, as I look at those four simple words, a voice somewhere in my head is telling me to erase them and say instead, "*If* I die . . ."

But that's an incomplete sentence, a tease. What's more, it's a cop-out and, yes, a lie. Because the truth is, I am going to die.

I don't have a dread disease. I'm not planning a dangerous adventure. And, despite the daily headlines, the odds that I could be caught in a natural disaster or a dramatic terrorist incident are really quite small.

So why think about death?

For one thing, the prospect of death is something I share with every living thing on this earth—with birds and bears, fish and bumblebees, roses and oak trees, with communists and contras, oil sheiks and waitresses, dentists and welfare recipients. And, of course, with each of you. Because regardless of whether you've ever forced yourself to write that sentence or even spoken the words quietly to yourself when you're alone, you—like me—are going to die.

There's another reason as well. Before that time comes, the chances are good that you or I will find ourselves dealing with the deaths of other people important to us. Except in rare cases, each of us first encounters death as a survivor. We learn about it by feeling and seeing its effects on ourselves and those around us.

That leads to a question: If death is something we all share and something we should prepare for, why are we so reluctant to talk about it, so unwilling to look it in the face: Is it really that ugly?

I have some theories, and I'm sure you do, too. But if you're like me, the questions about death outnumber the answers, despite the fact that great thinkers have pondered these issues from the time human beings discovered the question mark.

Death, mine and yours, is like the last sentence of a book. Some people say this sentence ends the story. Others believe the book has a sequel. Still others aren't really sure.

But these large questions don't exclude the smaller ones, the details we're sometimes ashamed (or afraid) to worry about beforehand because they seem trivial—questions about funerals, memorials, cremation, or burial. This book is meant to provide answers for those seemingly minor matters that are left to nag the living—the disposition of a body, planning a funeral or memorial service, expressing sympathy and, equally important, how to accept it. Then there's the matter of grief, how it gnaws on us, why it's important, and how the wounds of grief can heal.

It is only when we come to terms with death that we can make sense of the dilemmas that life presents. That's a lifetime's worth of work. But one way to start is simply by facing squarely the decisions and emotions that confront us when someone important to us dies.

In musing on death and the influence his understanding of mortality had on his music, the Russian composer Dmitri Shostakovich once said, "I think that if people began thinking about death sooner they'd make fewer foolish mistakes."

That's reason enough for this book.

Chapter 1

_____

When Words Come Hard

A friend is dying. What do you say to him?

Someone else has lost a loved one. What can you tell her?

Sometimes people take offense at the very words their would-be comforters consider the most appropriate: "I know how you feel."

I know grieving people who have bitterly resented hearing those words, or sentiments like them. I also know people who have found that kind of message immensely comforting.

What's wrong with saying, "I know how you feel"? And why is it sometimes right? Grieving people give us some clues:

A forty-year-old man in St. Petersburg, Florida, writes to tell how it feels to be dying of a terminal disease. He describes what it was like to fight his way twice out of a near-coma. In one crisis he was partially paralyzed for five weeks, enduring pain that "went beyond painkillers."

"I'd like to give you some advice," he writes. "Never say you can imagine what it must have been like to someone who has experienced a near-death situation. You can't imagine it; you just can't!"

He's right. The pain, the fear, the humiliation of losing bodily control—those feelings must be felt to be understood. We can't really "imagine" that pain. We can only offer our love and support to someone who has to go through it.

A woman in Los Angeles tells of the time she was returning home from her father's funeral in the Midwest. On a small commuter plane, she discovered to her dismay that she was seated next to a large, loquacious rancher—she was in no mood to talk to that type of person. So she took the initiative and explained to him that her father had just died, hoping that the confession would earn her some solitude.

To her surprise, he gently replied: "Well, my mother died last year. And a few years ago I lost my seventeen-year-old son. So I know something of what you're going through."

That, she says, was probably one of the most comforting things she heard in the first weeks of her grief. They talked throughout the flight about grief and how long it lasts, about death and about life.

"If he had said, 'I know how you feel,' I would have been furious," she says. "Instead, he said, 'I know *something* of what you're going through.' Even though he had had more deaths to deal with than I had, he didn't presume to know what my grief felt like to me.

"And yet," she adds, "in the months since my dad died, a close friend who lost her father a couple of years ago has said, 'I know how you feel' dozens of times and it doesn't offend me. She knew my father and how I felt about him, and I knew her father and how she felt about him. I think that's the difference."

The lesson here is that there are no rigid rules about *what* to say to a dying or grieving person. But there are good guidelines about *how* to say it.

Don't presume to know something about a person that you can't really know. And remember that your willingness to listen can be more important than anything you say.

Sometimes death comes so slowly, with such obvious wasting of a person's body, that friends may try to comfort the grieving family by suggesting that in this case death was a blessing.

If you are ever tempted to express that sentiment, here's some advice from a man who has been on the receiving end: don't.

David Lewis is a Baltimore man whose wife died after a long fight with ALS, the degenerative disease that afflicted Lou Gehrig. He kept a diary of his thoughts and reactions to events leading up to and following her death. Here are some excerpts from that diary,* used here with his permission:

"We had been grieving for over two years, increasingly so as the disease took its toll. Yet I was not ready for the overwhelm-

---
Journal of David Lewis, Copyright © 1988 by David Lewis.

ing grief that hit me as Jeannette was wheeled out of the apartment. There is no way to protect oneself against such a loss. It is true that, at last, Jeannette was released from the grip of that dreadful disease and that I was now free of the agony of seeing one I loved becoming a shell of herself. But it is deep, deep sorrow, not relief, that one feels at the moment of death and immediately following.

"It was only after I had a good cry that I began to feel a developing sense of relief for the two of us. Which leads me to make a major point with respect to those who offer condolences. After a person has had a long and difficult illness, people should not say, 'It was a blessed relief.' It is all right for the aggrieved one to think or say that the death provided relief for the patient, but those speaking to the mourner should just stick with: 'I am very sorry about your loss. Please accept my condolences.'

"To say that a death provides 'release' from a dreadful affliction is quite true, but it is inappropriate. It diminishes the sense of real loss and palpable grief that the mourner feels and is having a hard time handling. I felt like saying many times that if it was such a 'relief' why did I feel so rotten? . . . There is a considerable difference between feeling 'relieved' and being 'glad.' I was relieved that the hard struggle was over and that Jeannette had maintained her intellectual dignity and independence to the last, but I was not glad when she died!

". . . Jeannette and I were both ambivalent about her imminent departure. She wanted to 'go,' but at the same time she said, 'I do not want to leave you.' I wanted her to 'go' as well, but I also did not want to lose her, even at the end.

". . . The whole experience is much more complicated than 'Wasn't it a blessing?' I can say that, but I don't like others saying it!"

No matter how much of a struggle life becomes, the death of a loved one is never easy to accept, and grief can never be explained away. That's important to remember when offering comfort to bereaved friends.

What can you do when words seem inadequate? Try silence and a willingness to listen, suggests a woman in Tampa, Florida, who has lived through intense grief.

"Six years ago, my brother was hit and killed by a drunk driver," she writes. "He was twenty years old, I was fifteen. I have found that I love to talk about him. Anyone who will listen to me is helping me tremendously. I don't want the other person to say anything. I just want them to hear what I have to say about my brother. I can never talk too much about him."

She also includes a story which suggests another role silence can play, using your presence, rather than your words, to comfort a friend:

"When my friend Alice called, I heard the sadness in her voice. It was the first anniversary of her husband's death, she said, and she did not want to be alone. Could I come over?

"Alice opened the door and led me into her comfortable living room. She did not turn on a lamp to scatter the dusk, nor did she offer coffee. We sat down in opposite chairs. I was already thinking of comforting phrases, but I began by asking what I could do to help.

"She told me, 'I'd like you to sit quietly here. Be with me, not talking or anything, just be here.'

"I was a little deflated, having marshaled a string of uplifting phrases. Sit here? Why, anyone could do that.

"Alice closed her eyes and rocked gently in her chair. I watched her for a few minutes. Then, embarrassed by staring into a face that seemed so private, I began looking around the room at the familiar paintings, the polished furniture, the ornate rug. I felt tense and uncomfortable in the heavy silence.

"Alice continued to rock gently, her eyes closed. . . . I shifted in my chair, feeling increasingly awkward . . .

"Then, in the soft shadows, I began to let go of my own anxiety, surrendering to the silence which settled over us like a benign mist. My proud preoccupation with my own eagerness to talk ebbed as I slowly began to connect with Alice's needs. As I relaxed, I began to feel at one with her, began to understand the immensity of what I'd been asked to give to her: my presence.

"No lecture, no pep talk, no insightful platitudes, no recital of understanding. Just my presence.

"Calmness filled the darkening room as we sat together in silence. It was an hour, although it did not seem that long, before Alice opened her eyes and said simply, 'Thank you for coming. I'm all right now.'

"I smiled, rose, took her hands into mine and said, "I'll call you tomorrow.'"

When a friend is grieving, it's good to remember that comfort comes in more forms than just words.

Notes from the Heart—and Hand

Thirty years ago Frank E. Smith made a promise to himself. "I decided that never shall I send a commercial card, not for sorrow, nor to congratulate [for] birthday, graduation, birth of a child. NO CARD—EVER!"

He has kept that promise. From his home in Bayonet Point, Florida, Smith writes to tell me that his habit of sending friends a personal message rather than a preprinted sentiment has brought enormous pleasure and gratification, not just to the recipients but also to himself.

"I have written letters, composed single-pagers, two-pagers, little notes," he says. "Responses have indicated many were copied and mailed into the hundreds."

Some of them were framed, some were mounted on plaques, and one has even been bequeathed in a will from a father to a son as an "heirloom."

"I've been made so happy with what has happened," he says. "It gratifies my ego no end, but at the same time I think it's doing a lot of good."

Writing a personal note takes time, of course. But Smith

points out that, especially in times of sorrow, writing your thoughts down is in some ways easier than speaking with a bereaved person. Writing allows "time to think, to revise, to alter the power of your words," he says. Just "write right from the heart."

Frank Smith's writing habit has served him well—and never better than when his wife of forty years died after a long illness. At her memorial service friends received a copy of "Lee's Last Garden," described as "Storied moments from the life of Lena J. Smith, presented by her husband, Frank E. Smith."

The essay, about three typed pages, recounts the ways in which Lee created her own special beauty in and around the various homes the Smiths lived in during their years in Ohio and Florida.

I never knew Lee Smith, but reading her husband's recollections of big things and small, serious and funny, helped me picture the special habits and talents that must have made her a delightful woman. One story describes the "pretty good sized rock," Lee told Frank she was having installed in the small back-yard of their townhouse near Cleveland. "The fork-lift operators . . . had spent several hours 'putting the rock where the lady wanted it.' . . . There it was in our yard. Actually it was most of our yard," Frank writes.

"Well, my lady built a scene around that boulder, following Japanese principles. We had our own mountain scenery to look at from above as though we were in a plane . . . or [we could] sit at ground level and easily imagine those were far-off mountains. After a day or two she decided that I did like it, whereupon I was informed there had been some bribery. 'How much?' I asked. 'Couple bottles of Scotch.' I still liked it," he recalls, no doubt with a smile on his face.

After Lee's memorial service Smith says he needed more than seven hundred copies to fill requests.

Obviously, Frank Smith has a talent for words. But, as he points out, his tribute to Lee simply made use of a faculty we all have at our disposal—our memory. He suggests we use it more.

"Memory can comfort you in sorrow," he says. "Use it in a positive way. You've got enough pain. Review the happy times. Enjoy them over and over, as much as you feel you need to." As his own experience shows, if you put them in writing then other people can enjoy them too.

Condolence: It Goes Two Ways

Death has its own etiquette, and many of us are diligent about following the rules. We pay condolence calls, send flowers or food, write a note, and attend funerals or memorial services.

But how many people reach out a hand to grieving friends later on? A reader in Baltimore writes to tell of his experience befriending the elderly widow of a friend and colleague:

"A few years ago one of my best friends died, leaving his eighty-year-old widow at home with grown children far away. I had known George very well in our office and Joan less well. He was popular and active. She was retiring and a semi-invalid. His death was both expected and a shock for her after over a half-century of marriage.

"A detailed obituary pleased Joan and her children. Many colleagues visited her during the viewing. A friend gave a funeral tribute that moved many people to tears. The wake was a succession of colorful stories, fueled by love, good food, and good drink. Joan smiled often. The family stayed for several days.

"And then it was all over, the public mourning, the public party.

"I went back to visit Joan a week later and found her bereft. She had talked with no one for a couple of days. I had a drink or two and stayed for an hour. She picked up. We told stories about George. We told tales about our kids and her grandchildren. She gave me one of George's tweed sport coats and said come back.

"A week later I did. She was visibly happy to see me. She said her children kept in touch by phone, but sometimes she didn't have a visitor or a phone call for a day or two or three at a time. 'It's tough those days,' she said. 'A few of George's friends call but most don't.' We began to chat about things other than George. Ocean voyages she had taken as a young girl. Mountain hikes I had taken in the Rockies. Crazy people we had known, wild things we had done or dreamed of doing.

"In the coming months and for two years after, I saw Joan often. So did a few of George's colleagues and periodically her children from out of town. We visited mostly at her home. Once in a while I picked her up in my car, and we went for rides. One wonderful evening we went to the symphony.

"It was a great friendship. When she died, it was both expected and a shock for me.

"I wore George's coat to her funeral, but thought mainly of Joan and our friendship of the last two years.

"After a death is over and the needed funeral etiquette is done, and the friends fade away and forget, that's the time to remember the living and come back.

"A week later. Two weeks later. Three weeks later. Months later. That's when the living want a letter and a call on the telephone, a knock on the door, a smile, some stories."

As this man learned, reaching out to comfort other people is not a one-way street. It can spark a continuing friendship in which comfort and kindness go both ways.

Not always, though. Here's an example of an act of friendship that did not bring as rewarding a response:

Q: "I wrote what I thought was a very feeling letter of sympathy to the widow of an old friend who had died recently. All I got back was a printed thank you card with just the widow's name on it, nothing else. I felt a little unappreciated and even embarrassed that I had written her so emotionally. Am I overly sensitive?"—E.P., Durham, North Carolina

A: Your question shows why rules of etiquette exist. The rituals of giving and receiving sympathy may seem arbitrary—

writing to acknowledge such a letter is probably not what many grieving people really feel like doing.

Yet there is a reason for acknowledging acts of sympathy, and your question is a good reminder of that. When we reach out to someone who has lost a loved one, especially when we take time to express our thoughts in a very personal way, we are taking an emotional risk. What if we look silly? Will our feelings really matter to that person?

Even worse, what if the letter you put so much of yourself into simply got lost in the mail, leaving the widow to think you didn't care enough to acknowledge an old friend's death?

Having reached out to someone, you naturally want assurance, first of all, that your letter was delivered. Ideally, you would also like to know that it provided some comfort to the widow, or reminded her that she is not alone in this time of grief.

The preprinted acknowledgment you received at least lets you know that your letter arrived, and, frankly, that's probably more acknowledgment than many acts of sympathy get these days. But obviously you felt you deserved a more personal response.

That said, never doubt that your letter was appreciated. Acts of kindness in a time of crisis are never a waste of time or effort, and you certainly have no reason to be embarrassed for expressing your feelings about an old friend.

In times of grief some people may simply be incapable of taking pen in hand, or they may not feel capable of expressing their feelings in their own words. Even though it is natural for us to want recognition or response when we reach out to others, it is important to remember that the most meaningful acts of kindness or sympathy are those that are voluntary. We choose to do them regardless of the response.

Even so, your question provides a good lesson for anyone who ever has or will be on the receiving end of condolences. Of course we deserve sympathy in times of grief. But sympathy has its best effects when it's based on good communication—and communication goes two ways.

How should we acknowledge expressions of sympathy? Ideally, all responses should be handwritten. Realistically, however, it's hard to condemn sending a preprinted acknowledgment or the commercial sympathy cards which people often substitute for condolence letters. They are better than nothing.

But for more personal acts of kindness, such as flowers or personal letters, a handwritten note is a reasonable expectation. It needn't be long; one or two sentences would do: "Thank you for your kindness. Your friendship means a great deal to me."

That's enough to let our friends know their support is important. And it's enough to remind us that it's not just good manners to acknowledge our friends' kindnesses; it's also good therapy.

Here's another case of tangled etiquette in the days after a death:

Q: "Three years ago when my mother passed away, my sister-in-law was gracious enough to assist me in sending acknowledgments. We took turns reading addresses, and my turn for writing the envelopes was first. When we decided to switch, my sister-in-law said, 'Why are you giving me their names? They didn't send flowers or a memorial contribution.' I said that it didn't matter; they were good enough to come to the funeral home. She said that didn't make any difference—they weren't entitled to an acknowledgment. I was appalled, and so was my father when he overheard this.

"I'm wondering how many others have this same attitude? Perhaps it would be an interesting discussion topic."—A.G., Dearborn, Michigan

A: I suspect plenty of people share your sister-in-law's attitude, and that's too bad. Think of it this way: If we send an acknowledgment only to people who are "entitled" to it, aren't we really asking people to "earn" our gratitude?

Certainly in times of grief or crisis, some friends will be more stalwart than others. Yet, as you know, in those times every expression of sympathy and support can mean a great deal.

The notion that there is some arbitrary cutoff point for expressions of gratitude goes against the spirit of friendship and compassion that death elicits in friends and acquaintances.

Moreover, it ignores another aspect of human nature—the fact that we need other people to help us through the times of grief, loneliness, or even despondency that can linger for months or sometimes even years after the death of a loved one. An expression of gratitude to friends encourages further acts of friendship.

Grief is a wrenching experience, and it doesn't end with the funeral. That's why the rules of etiquette that demand thank-you notes in the first place make sense psychologically.

Like visitation, funerals, and the other rituals surrounding death, the process—or chore, if you like—of acknowledging acts of friendship and sympathy are good therapy. They provide another way of coming to terms with a loss, as well as another way of giving perspective to the life of the person we are grieving.

It's also important to remember that personal expressions of sympathy—letters, notes, or visits—can cost more in emotional terms than flowers or memorial contributions. That's why they are equally deserving of a written response.

This letter, from a teenaged girl in Florida, is proof of the need people have to reach out to the family of a friend who is near death or has died. This need is especially great for young people, for whom death should, in a better world, be a distant stranger.

Q. "I have a friend who was in an automobile accident almost two weeks ago. They say she is in a coma, not responding to anything. I wanted to see her, but only the family is allowed in. I believe her mother doesn't want to see anyone, especially teen-agers. You see, my friend was riding in a car and a fourteen-year-old was driving. Of course, my friend was the one seriously hurt.

"I have tried calling the family and I went to the hospital, but I can't get any more information.

"Do you know what else I can do? I thought maybe I could see my friend, talk to her, just let her know I am there. Or do you think I am being too pushy? Is it good for a teenager to see a friend who had so much life in her all of a sudden be on all kinds of machines to keep her alive? I truly have mixed emotions. I want to see my friend, yet I am afraid.

"Also, have you ever heard of a city-wide teenage prayer vigil? I am sure there are teenagers who would pray if only there was notice of the special day."

A. First of all, you should know that even though you do not qualify as a family member, you are an important part of your friend's life. If she does survive, your friendship will become even more important in helping her overcome her injuries.

In the meantime is there someone—your parents, a counselor, or a good friend—with whom you can discuss your own reactions to the accident? Families need sympathy and support in times like this, but so do friends like you.

It is only natural for you to want to reach out to your friend's family, but it is important to realize that they are still stunned that tragedy could strike so suddenly. I suspect they are also exhausted from the physical strain of spending long hours at the hospital and from the emotional strain of seeing their daughter in this condition.

In times like this, it is important to respect a family's need for privacy. But that doesn't mean there is nothing you can do. For starters, you could send your friend a card telling her how much you are thinking of her. Even though she won't be able to read it, it will let her family know of your concern. It would be nice to include a note to them as well.

If your friend remains in the hospital and moves out of intensive care, you may want to find a special object to send her to brighten up her room, perhaps a small stuffed animal that could be placed on her bed or on a bedside table. You may even want to give it a special name and include a note explaining that you hope it will remind her of all her friends and their good wishes for her.

If she stays in a coma you may never know whether she is aware of any of your expressions of friendship. But you can take comfort in knowing that if there is any possibility that she is conscience of her surroundings, she will know that her friends have not forgotten her.

As for a visit, certainly it will be a shock to see her in that condition. But if you still want to do it and the family agrees, remind yourself that you're doing this for her, not just for you. That will help to put your own feelings in perspective.

You mention the possibility of a prayer vigil. That could be a good way to do something for your friend and her family during these tense days when you feel so cut off from her. If you are active in a church, perhaps you could ask the pastor or youth advisor to help you organize a vigil. Your friends in church or other youth organizations may also want to help.

Meanwhile, you may want to talk to your school guidance counselor, who can perhaps get more information about your friend's condition. Your counselor can also help you and your friends deal with your own grief about the accident, and perhaps even help all of you explore ways to show your friend and her family that your thoughts and best wishes are with them.

Chapter 2

Helping Children Understand Death

When families gather after a death, one characteristic seems to hold true: however somber the adults may be, young children, after a while, cannot resist the urge to scamper around, play and, in general, act like children.

That's because they *are* children, and their reactions to grief don't match those of adults. That doesn't mean children don't feel grief or know that something sad or final or tragic has occurred.

Children are highly attuned to the emotions of the people around them. But they grieve in their own way, and it's important that adults recognize a child's need for honesty, love, and reassurance when death occurs.

As many as 5 percent of all children—1.5 million or so— experience the death of one or both parents by the time they are fifteen. Many other children lose siblings, close friends, or grandparents.

But the frequency with which death invades young lives does not make it less painful. And all too often, children confronting death for the first time are doing so along with adults who are immersed or even immobilized by grief.

Sometimes adults' preoccupation with grief prevents them from seeing that a child's reaction to death is just as deep as theirs—even though it may be expressed differently, depending on the child's age and stage of emotional development.

Unlike adults, who can sustain a continuous, prolonged stage of grieving, young children are more likely to exhibit their grief in spurts, perhaps over a period of several years. Just as adults react differently to grief, children also express their feelings in very personal ways.

Sometimes those expressions can startle adults. It's common for young children who lose a parent or sibling to resume playing soon after the death, as if nothing has happened. They may also make statements that seem glib to adults and ask the same questions over and over.

They may act in aggressive or hostile ways and seem not to care about the death. Within a few weeks, they may begin asking when the family will get a replacement for the lost parent or sibling.

When this happens, it's important for adults to remember that intense emotions are hard for young children to sustain. In these situations it's common for children to show "approach and avoidance" behavior—approaching the loss, then backing away from the painful reality of what it means. That's understandable, otherwise the reality of death would be too overwhelming to face.

Adults should recognize this process and allow a child the chance to grieve. Psychologists point out that what other people may regard as a child's "quick recovery" from the death of a family member may only signal more problems later on. Denying grief does not make it go away. On the other hand, children have a natural resilience. Studies of grieving adults have long noticed that more physical aches and pains crop up in the months following the loss of a close relative. However, recent studies of grieving children have shown that adults should not dismiss such complaints from them as merely being grief-related. In many of these cases, children really are sick when they complain.

However, children who are experiencing grief do need a special measure of attention and support, especially when the death is in the immediate family. Teachers should acknowledge the loss in an appropriate way. Some teachers have done this by presenting a book to the child on her first day back. Another possibility is a certificate saying that the class has made a contribution to some charity in honor of the child's loved one. These presentations break the ice, and make it easier for classmates to express their support and sympathy.

Adults should be especially aware of a characteristic that all human beings seem to share—the tendency to feel guilty about a death. It's especially important to reassure children that the death is not their fault, that their loved one did not die because of something the child did or failed to do.

How do you help a young child understand death? Not by waiting till the day Granddaddy dies to try to explain such an overwhelming reality.

Children as young as four years old should be taught about death and are capable of understanding the basic concepts.

The death of a friend or relative can be a terrifying experience for a young child. Yet often young children will seem to grasp the reality of death at one moment, only to skip off the next minute to play.

When death does claim someone they know, ignorance can result in deep-seated fears and confusion. Imagine, for instance, something that could scare any child (or adult, too, for that matter)—a poster for a horror movie showing a hand digging its way out of a grave. Less obvious to an adult is a common description given to children about death, that Grandmother simply "went to sleep." To adults that sounds peaceful. For a child, it can turn bedtime into a nightmare.

The same is true when children are told that a relative who has died has simply "gone on a long journey." What are they supposed to think when Mommy leaves home in the morning or if Daddy has an overnight business trip?

Children who have lost a friend or relative may not have the words to describe their fears. In many cases, they act them out in disruptive behavior.

Drawing from his work with bereaved children, Dr. David J. Schonfeld, a fellow in behavioral and developmental pediatrics at the University of Maryland School of Medicine, designed a study to determine whether children between the ages of four and eight could understand the complicated ideas associated with death. Through films, stories, and discussions, students were introduced to the key concepts:

—The irreversibility of death. Unlike an absent person who is simply away on a trip, a dead person will not return.

—The finality of death. When death occurs, life functions cease in the body. When children don't understand this, they may worry that a buried relative is cold, hungry, in pain, or may need to go to the bathroom. (David Techner, a funeral director in Southfield, Michigan, says that the two most frequent questions about caskets he gets from children are: "Where are Granddad's legs?" and "Where's the bathroom?"—meaning the bathroom for the casket. Children often approach questions about death far more literally than adults do.)

—The inevitability of death. No living thing can escape death forever. Children may view significant people in their lives as immune to death. Or, unless they understand that death comes to everyone eventually, they may see it as a punishment, perhaps for something the child did or said. This could lead to feelings of excessive guilt or shame.

—The causes of death. Children who do not have a realistic understanding of the causes of death can resort to fantasy or magical thinking. As a result, they end up believing that their own bad thoughts or actions caused the death.

Dr. Schonfeld found that after a series of six, thirty-to-forty-five-minute programs over a three-week period, the children understood concepts that would normally have taken them a year to grasp. He also found that children were eager to talk about death, to ask questions and tell their own experiences. Too often, though, adults aren't willing to listen.

They should. As Dr. Schonfeld points out, "You can't take away the sadness, but you can help with the adjustment."

Using Stories to Explain Death

One way to introduce children to the idea of death is through books. Children love stories, and not just because they help to prolong bedtime. Whether recalled from a grandfather's boyhood, made up by an imaginative mother or read from a favorite book, stories help teach little people who they are, why they are, and how they fit into the world around them. Since that world is one that includes death, stories become an important way for a child to make sense of life, of the rhythms that bring birth and growth and also death. It's easy to say that death is a fact of life. But facts don't explain much to tender hearts, whether they are four years old or forty. Stories are much better at getting an important point across.

A classic example is *Charlotte's Web*, by E.B. White (with delightful illustrations by Garth Williams), first published in 1952. It's recommended for older preschool children up through about the third grade, but plenty of older children and adults are enchanted by this simple story.

Charlotte, you will recall, is a spider who spins her web in a barn owned by Mr. Homer L. Zuckerman, uncle of eight-year-old Fern Arable. Fern lives on a nearby farm, and we meet her early one morning as she saves a little pig from her father's ax, a common fate for the runt of a large litter.

Fern names her pig Wilbur and lavishes on him food and affection. When he grows too big for Fern to keep, Uncle Homer buys him and Wilbur moves to the Zuckermans' barn.

Soon Wilbur learns from the other animals that pigs born in the spring are often killed and eaten at Christmastime. He is terrified by this news, but his wise new friend, Charlotte the spider, promises that somehow she'll save him from this awful fate.

She does. Through the magic of her web, she persuades the Zuckermans and neighbors for miles around that Wilbur is "some pig," that he's "terrific" and even "radiant."

People are sure that spiders can't write, so they take the

appearance of these words in Charlotte's web as a miraculous sign, and Wilbur in fact becomes a terrific and radiant pig worthy of a special medal at the state fair, a pig too valuable to kill for bacon or ham. The words in Charlotte's web save Wilbur's life.

She goes with him to the state fair and spins one more web, announcing that this terrific pig is also "humble." But just at his moment of glory, the time comes for Charlotte to spin her greatest work, her egg sac. She then tells Wilbur that she is too weak to go back to the Zuckermans' barn. "Wilbur leapt to his feet. 'Not going back?' he cried. 'Charlotte, what are you talking about?'

"'I'm done for,' she replied. 'In a day or two I'll be dead. I haven't even strength enough to climb down into the crate. . . .'"

"Hearing this, Wilbur threw himself down in an agony of pain and sorrow. Great sobs racked his body. He heaved and grunted with desolation. 'Charlotte,' he moaned. 'Charlotte! My true friend!'"

Wilbur can't save Charlotte, but he does save her children, gently carrying her egg sac back to the barn where he guards it throughout the long, cold winter. Next spring, to his delight, hundreds of Charlotte's children emerge. Most of them leave, but three stay to keep him company. The pattern continues spring after spring.

As Wilbur learns about the passage of the seasons, that love can be interrupted by loss, or that loneliness can melt into contentment and even joy, young readers begin to learn these lessons as well. Wilbur loses his best friend, but her gift makes it possible for him to live a full life.

Wilbur discovers that through her children, Charlotte leaves something of herself in this world. And yet she is unique, unlike any other spider or any other friend. Wilbur learns that he can't replace Charlotte, but that in his own way he can repay her gift.

"Wilbur never forgot Charlotte," E.B. White tells us. "Although he loved her children and grandchildren dearly, none of the new spiders ever quite took her place in his heart. She was in a class by herself. It is not often that someone comes along who is a true friend and a good writer. Charlotte was both."

Answer Their Questions

Good stories teach valuable lessons. But don't expect children to digest those lessons without plenty of questions.

During one classroom discussion a first-grader asked: "How does my body know when it's time to die?"

This young boy was doing what all children do at one time or another. He was seeking factual information about a subject that seems to turn even the most matter-of-fact adult into an armchair philosopher, ready to give the child every kind of explanation except the one he needs most.

Often, questions about death turn into those occasions when adults need to step back a moment and think about the question from a child's point of view, before jumping in with an answer more appropriate to an adult than to a first-grader.

Dr. Kathleen McCarty, a psychiatrist who heads the Supportive Services Team for terminally ill patients and their families at the UCLA Medical Center, suggests some guidelines. First, she says, it's a good idea to think about what may have prompted the question.

As it turns out, in this case the boy had recently lost a grandparent. The death of a family member, or of anyone the child knows, will prompt questions that deserve appropriate answers from adults. Dr. McCarty suggests that adults be both specific and accurate. Above all, she says, they should address the concerns that are uppermost in the child's mind.

When children confront a reality as big as death, it's natural for their next thought to be centered on themselves: "What about *me?* If Grandpa died, am I going to die, too?" (Adults wonder the same thing, but we've learned, for better or worse, not to ask so many questions.) Next, they will wonder about the people they're closest to—usually their parents: "If Grandpa died and left me, will Mommy or Daddy die and leave me, too?"

Children's worries about death can be compounded by the explanations they get from adults. For instance, if a child is told that Grandmother "went to sleep," the child might worry that if she goes to sleep, she'll die, too. Or if the first grader was told that his grandfather died because he was tired or sick—both of which could have been true—he might worry the next time he hears Daddy say he's really tired, or the next time Mom complains she isn't feeling too well that day.

"Always address the fears the child has about death for himself and those who take care of him," Dr. McCarty says. Explain to the child that "the way that person felt weak or tired is different from the way we feel weak or tired."

Which brings us back to that simple but mysterious question: "How will my body know when it's time to die?"

"Bodies do know," says Dr. McCarty, who in her work has seen many people meet death. She points to animals as an example that will help children to understand that when we use words like "weak" or "tired" to explain death, we're not talking about the way we feel tired at bedtime, or how we feel when we have a cold or even the flu.

"Animals go off and curl up. They let you know when they're ready to die," Dr. McCarty says. "People go through the same thing."

The boy's questions caught the adults in the classroom that day by surprise. And no wonder. Death is not a simple question for adults; it triggers many other questions and associations. When a child asks for facts on "how" we know it's time to die, the adult is probably busy wondering, more philosophically, "whether" we know when it's time to die.

When you're old enough to understand something about the loss that death involves, and when you know how final it is, it's harder to speak of the moment life leaves our bodies in a way that sounds as casual as mentioning what time dinner will be served. Yet for children the question comes naturally.

It helps when adults can with equal ease provide answers that include the factual information asked for and also address the fears that are often lurking behind the questions.

Chapter 3

When the Loved One Isn't Human

One of the most biting satirical treatments of the pomp and circumstance that is often associated with American funerals was Evelyn Waugh's novel, *The Loved One,* set in Los Angeles in the early part of the century. The "loved one" was one cemetery's way of referring to the bodies of the deceased, bodies that were assumed to deserve all the care and cosmetics, all the emotion and sentiment that would be accorded the wealthiest movie star. Much of the story's humor comes from the fact that the "loved ones" at this cemetery were not people at all, but rather the pets of the rich and famous.

We all know that there are cases in which animals are given better treatment than humans. That's just as true in life as it is in death. And yet the fact that some people react to the death of animals in ways that strike others as inappropriate need not obscure the real sense of loss that people feel when they lose a well-loved animal.

A friend once confessed to me that when his cat died he grieved for months, but that when his mother died a few years later he seemed to recover much sooner. He felt odd about that because he loved his mother very deeply.

His mother lived in another city, and he had known for several months that she had a terminal illness. Even so, he wondered whether his emotions were upside down. Did he care more about an animal, no matter how special, than his own mother?

We talked about it for a while, noting that the cat had been a part of his daily routine for more than fifteen years. The cat had stayed with him through a marriage and a divorce. She had been the stable point in his life when he changed apartments, careers, and cities. She was, in effect, his family. It seemed natural that he would grieve when she died.

His mother's death affected him in deeper and larger ways.

But the loss of his cat was something he noticed in little ways every day.

If people grieve for animals, how should their friends react? Is the death of a pet a reason for a condolence call or a sympathy note? Common sense tells us that friends will always appreciate thoughtfulness at such a time.

A wonderful example of such kindness is found in *The Letters of Edith Wharton,* edited by R.W.B. and Nancy Lewis and published by Charles Scribner's Sons. Wharton, who died in 1937, was not only the author of elegant fiction, but also a prolific writer of delightful letters and notes to friends.

She was also a dog-lover, and when she and her husband, Teddy, learned of the death of Taffy, who belonged to their friend, Charles Eliot Norton, she sent this note:

"When Teddy and I heard yesterday from Lily of Taffy's sad taking-off we both really felt a personal regret in addition to our profound sympathy for his master.

"His artless but engaging ways, his candid enjoyment of his dinner, his judicious habit of exercising by means of those daily rushes up and down the road, had for so many years interested and attracted us that he occupies a very special place in our crowded dog-memories.

"As for your feelings, I can picture them with intensity, since to do so I have only to relive my poor Jules' last hours and farewell looks, about a year ago!

". . . Staunch and faithful little lovers that they are, they give back a hundred fold every sign of love one ever gives them and it mitigates the pang of losing them to know how very happy a little affection has made them.

"Teddy joins me in condolences . . ."

Without sentimentalizing Taffy, Edith Wharton conveyed genuine sympathy to her friend, while according to Taffy all the respect and affection good and loyal dogs deserve.

More recently, the death of an animal brought the kind of response Edith Wharton would never dream of—a press release.

Usually the flood of announcements from Capitol Hill offices are predictable: "Congressman Smith takes credit for new road building funds," "Senator Jones denounces budget deficit"—you get the picture.

But one summer weekend, Representative Les Aspin of Wisconsin produced a nine-paragraph, nonpolitical press release that deserves notice:

"Saturday, August 26, 1989, Washington, D.C.—Rep. Les Aspin today announced the death of his longtime canine companion, Junket.

"Junket, a sheepdog mix, aged fourteen, had been suffering from arthritis, digestive troubles and other infirmities associated with old age. She died Saturday, August 19 . . ."

Now some taxpayers may see that as one more example of waste, fraud, and abuse in Congress. A press release-obituary for a dog?

As it happens, Junket was one of a handful of "working" dogs on Capitol Hill, dogs who accompany their owner-congressmen to the office.

Some dogs work as guides or helpers for blind or disabled people. Others earn their keep by herding sheep or cattle, by tracking game or by using their extraordinary noses in detective work.

And many dogs, like Junket, provide a valuable service simply by being themselves, in this case, providing companionship and continuity to a Congressman living on his own. In the process, they probably overcome as many barriers as a seeing-eye dog.

According to the press release, "Junket was delighted with children and adults alike and showed no bias between Democrats and Republicans—although in one brief digression from good behavior she deposited a sign of visitation on the doorstep of Louisiana Republican David Treen's office. Treen later left to become governor of Louisiana."

Junket, rescued from an animal shelter in 1975 by Rep. Aspin's former wife, also served as the congressman's campaign mascot, and her picture appeared on the T-shirts and mugs presented to campaign volunteers. In Washington, she served as the "premier greeter" for the office—ensuring, no doubt, that visitors weren't bored while waiting to see the congressman.

Junket sounds like a big bundle of nonpartisan friendliness, something sorely lacking on Capitol Hill. I'm sure she is missed and, yes, I think her death was worth a press release.

More than most dogs, Junket lived a public life. But anyone who has lived with an animal knows the emotional hold a pet can have on a human. And because the life expectancy of a dog or cat is less than ours, most pet owners at one time or another have to deal with the death of a pet. Yet, too often friends or coworkers take the attitude, "Well, it was just an animal. You can always get another."

But whether they "work" or not, pets become an important part of our lives. We come to know and love them as companions, as creatures with their own distinct habits and personalities. They also come to know us and, despite all our shortcomings, they do more than put up with us—they even like us. No wonder we mourn their deaths.

It's true that pets aren't people. But it's not true that they are interchangeable, that losing a pet is something we can or should shrug off as trivial.

The death of an animal is often a child's first encounter with loss and grief, and plenty of children hold "funerals" for their dogs or cats before they ever attend a service marking a human death.

For children and adults alike the loss of a pet can further the process of understanding death intellectually and emotionally. Pausing to mark the death of a pet who has given its human friends years of unconditional affection is not a frivolous act, but a worthwhile step in coming to terms with death.

At such times, notes, sympathetic comments or other acts of kindness acknowledging a friend's loss are entirely appropriate.

Chapter 4

Death and Holidays

Even in holiday seasons, when peace and joy are supposed to fill the air, there are many households where the outer trappings of celebration have been wrenched into a different perspective. These are the homes where a family member is terminally ill, celebrating what everyone knows will be his or her last holiday.

How do you celebrate in the face of death? Dr. Kathleen McCarty, director of UCLA's Supportive Services Team for terminally ill patients and their families, has some helpful advice.

"Holidays are especially hard when you know it's the last one with a family member," Dr. McCarty says. "That holiday will forever be colored by the death of that person and it can be very difficult for the family in the years ahead."

Dr. McCarty encourages patients and their families to make the holiday a special time, so that the family will have memories other than tragedy and loss to look back on.

At Christmas, for example, the imminent death of a loved one exposes the shallowness of the materialism we have come to associate with that season. It forces families to rely on their deepest values, to recognize that life is a precious gift and that their relationships with each other are far more important than a brightly wrapped box under a perfect tree.

She usually suggests to patients that they make a special gift for their families, something that doesn't take a lot of effort but that lets them know how important they are to the patient. Letters to family members would hold a great deal of value, as would tape-recorded messages, needlework, or other small projects that a patient could undertake.

Is a parent dying before the children are old enough to have asked questions about their father's childhood or wondered about their mother's hopes and dreams? A tape could be made without too much exertion and in short intervals. Over the years, it would take on great value for the child.

Dr. McCarty cautions families to include patients when making plans. Don't assume you know how they want to spend the holiday. Ask them how *they* want to make the day special. Don't exclude them from holiday activities. Let them watch the tree trimming or participate in Christmas carols if they feel like it.

Most problems families face at such times are not from the immediate household, Dr. McCarty says, but rather from other family members who may be arriving for special visits. They should be encouraged to be natural, not to exude artificial optimism or cut the patient off if she wants to tell them how much they mean to her or to talk about her thoughts about death.

Dying people are acutely able to enjoy precious moments and their last holidays can contain their own kind of joy—but not the kind we so often try to achieve through a compulsion to have everything perfect. Families facing death know that the real meaning of a holiday such as Christmas is the love they have for each other.

Changing Your Routine

"November 14, 1985—two words blew my world apart: inoperable cancer. What was there to be thankful for?"

For Jeannene T., a reader in Joppa, Maryland, Thanksgiving had always been the holiday when her scattered family made a special effort to get together. So her husband's diagnosis of terminal cancer, coming only days before the holiday, has made that day especially hard for her in the years since his death.

Holidays weren't made for grief. There comes a time for most of us when the festivity only sharpens the pain of a recent death.

When that happens, we cope in different ways. There are no firm rules for helping grieving people face the holidays, only suggestions or guidelines that other people have found helpful.

Sometimes, as in this case, one particular holiday will carry especially painful associations with the death. But the task of the living is to carry on. Here is how this woman and her family have done that, beginning with the Thanksgiving when her husband was still alive:

"We canceled plans to travel to Ohio and spend Thanksgiving with our youngest child and her new husband. We made new plans; all three of our children and their spouses would spend Thanksgiving at our home.

"Because my husband was too sick to come to dinner, we set up the video camera, and he watched the dinner table from his bed. How did we cope? With laughter. We recalled old memories that were fun and spoke them out loud. We added outlandish comments about the way our son was carving the turkey, and all in all ignored the terror that was growing in each of us.

"Thanksgiving Day in 1986 was worse. How can you be thankful when your spouse died in April? Life goes on, but things must change. It was the first Thanksgiving without my husband, and I spent the weekend with my sister. Sure, this brought back old-time memories, but it was not too successful.

"Try again, do something different, I thought. So in 1987 I did just that. On Thanksgiving Day I did something that shocked a few people. This grandmother did not bake or cook or anything. For the first time in my life I spent Thanksgiving Day eating out.

"A single female friend and I took my youngest child and her husband to a dinner theater. I am not sure it was the right answer, but it did make the day a little easier because there was something else to focus our attention on.

"I don't know if this is a way for others to cope, but it helped me. The next year I drove to Virginia Beach to spend the weekend with my oldest daughter, her husband, and my granddaughter. I didn't know if that would help. I wasn't sure that I wasn't running away. As it turned out, my daughter invited a couple with two young children to join us. With strangers you can't just retreat. I was forced into being congenial. It helped to do that.

"I think that the best thing is to do something—even if it doesn't prove totally satisfying."

As this woman discovered, a good way to deal with holidays after a painful loss is to make a new tradition. After all, you can't go back.

Acknowledging Grief

Holidays are the time to bring out the greeting card list, and add a few names or change a few addresses. The ritual of sending and receiving holiday cards can be as rewarding as friendship itself.

But what happens when a couple on your list is no longer a couple, but instead a grieving spouse? Or when a family has lost a parent or even a child? Are holiday greetings—expressions we associate with a happy time of year—appropriate for friends who are mourning a death?

The short answer is yes—as long as the greetings are appropriate.

In fact, counselors who work with grieving people say they need to be remembered at holiday times, especially if remembering them includes acknowledging their grief.

Rather than just sending the cheerful greetings you're mailing to most people on your list, it may be more appropriate to write a short note or include a few sentences on a tasteful or comforting card.

Your message doesn't have to be long or complicated. Here is one example: "I've heard that holidays are especially difficult for people who have lost a loved one, and I wanted you to know I'm thinking about you."

The important thing is to let your friends know that you haven't forgotten their grief or the person who died. Memories are always important, but especially so at holidays.

One of the painful feelings that comes with grief is the fear that a loved one who has died will be forgotten. That's why it's important not to be afraid to mention that person's name to the survivors, to let them know you remember, too.

Your note might say something like: "I bet this isn't an easy time for you. We just want you to know that we're remembering Jane, too, and wishing peace and comfort for you."

Death isn't the only kind of loss people face, and it can be helpful to friends for you to acknowledge their divorce or separation as well. Again, the important thing is to let them know you realize the holidays may not be an easy time, and assure them of your continued friendship and support.

A word of caution: Don't assume that every grieving person will have a miserable holiday. Each person grieves in a different way.

Some people will find holidays painful; others may discover that, with so much going on, they actually enjoy the holidays. They shouldn't have to feel guilty for that.

Your role as a friend is not to presume to know how they should feel, but to let them know that however they deal with the holidays, you care about them and they have your love and support.

Recalling Memories

The same reasons that can make holidays so special can also make them especially painful for people still grieving for a loved one who has died.

Holidays intensify feelings, whether they are feelings of happiness and joy, irritation at minor annoyances, or a deep sense of grief and loss.

"Holidays and all anniversaries are difficult," says Elizabeth Haase, coordinator of training at the St. Francis Center in Washington, D.C., an organization that works with grieving people and those with life-threatening illnesses. Since people experience grief in such individual ways, Ms. Haase prefers to give general guidelines rather than specific suggestions for the holidays.

It's important, Ms. Haase says, to recognize that holidays will affect your feelings in some way. If the death is recent, you may feel much sadder and more depressed than on other days. You may cry a lot and feel tremendous anguish on holidays and anniversaries during the year after a death.

Yet what catches some people off guard is the grief that may crop up when the loss is not so recent. "People often tell me on the second anniversary of a death that they thought the first year would be the worst, but that they are finding the second year even harder," Ms. Haase says. "That often comes as a shock. They expect to feel better the second year, but it doesn't always happen.

"Allow those memories to be there," she adds. "Recognize that you may feel that way, but also that you may not."

That's the thing we often forget about human emotions— they're not predictable, and, deep down, we wouldn't really want them to be. On the other hand, being ambushed by our feelings can be a wrenching experience, especially at a festive time of year.

There are times when we're surprised by the intensity of our grief, or the fact that we're overwhelmed by memories even though we thought we had come to terms with the death. But there can also be times when we're surprised by the absence of pain. We may begin to enjoy ourselves, and then suddenly feel guilty that we're not sad. "Sometimes you feel you're betraying the person who died by having a good time," Ms. Haase says.

When that happens, "You should let yourself feel what you feel. Everybody grieves in different ways," she says. That's an important part of coming to terms with death.

It's also important for other people to give you "permission to grieve," Ms. Haase says. Sometimes that can be as simple as allowing you to mention the name of the person who has died, tell a story about him or her, or recall a part of the holiday that he or she particularly enjoyed. Grieving people often say that even though remembering their loved one can be painful, it's equally painful for other people to make no mention of them at all.

Holidays are not a time to forget those who have died, but rather to incorporate memories of them into occasions that celebrate the continuity and richness of life.

Chapter 5

Learning to Survive

In an essay on rural funerals in *The Sketch Book* (1819–20), Washington Irving observed: "The sorrow for the dead is the only sorrow from which we refuse to be divorced. Every other wound we seek to heal, every other affliction to forget; but this wound we consider it a duty to keep open, this afflication we cherish and brood over in solitude."

Grief, however painful, keeps us acutely conscious of the deceased. In that sense it helps to keep that person alive in our hearts and minds. Holding onto grief is a way of protesting the possibility that time will dull the sharp edges of our memory, robbing us further of the presence of a lost loved one.

Q: "I would imagine my question is often asked, although to me it is pertinent and original. Perhaps there is no simple answer.

"How does one cope with the passing of a loved one? How, after forty-five years of marriage, of sharing, loving, and solving life's problems together, can I learn to accept her passing and get on with life, as I am so often told I must do? In the final analysis, I guess I am asking how you say goodbye to a part of you, to a love that withstood the vicissitudes of life through youth and maturity.

"I have thought of support groups, but all I hear, in a dispassionate way, is 'Now it is time for me to get on with my life,' or 'I must accept death as the extension of life.' However, no one tells you how to accept, how to get on with life. Perhaps there is no cathartic—only time."—A.L., Baltimore

A: There is no simple, painless answer to such wrenching grief. When a partnership has lasted almost half a century, well-meaning advice to "get on with life" can sound hollow, trivial, and even cruel.

Yet, it's also true that time does bring some respite. After all, your wife has died, but you have not. Surviving means that at some point you do embrace life again.

In doing so, you know that the life you build will not be the same. But that does not mean you cannot make it worthwhile. You may never again experience peace or contentment in exactly the same way. But that is not to say you will never again smile at a joke or enjoy a sunset or perk up when the birds sing. That may not happen this week or this month. What is important is not the timetable for your grief (each person's is different), but that you understand your need to grieve—and grieve deeply— for a time. Grief hurts, but it also helps you heal.

No matter how many people have survived a similar loss, your grief is as unique as your own life, your wife's life, and the relationship you built day-by-day, through forty-five years of marriage. Yet it's remarkable how many grieving people find that when they describe their feelings, other people respond, recognizing instantly the kind of pain they felt themselves.

"There is a sort of invisible blanket between the world and me," wrote the English scholar and author C.S. Lewis soon after the death of his wife, Joy. "I find it hard to take in what anyone says. Or perhaps, hard to want to take it in. It is so uninteresting. Yet I want the others to be about me. . . . If only they would talk to one another and not to me."

That description comes from a journal Lewis kept, later published as *A Grief Observed.* You might profit from reading this slender book. You may also find it helpful to keep your own journal. Writing down your thoughts and feelings can help you come to terms with the new reality of your life and help preserve your memories of your wife.

You may find that you want to talk about your wife but that relatives and friends feel awkward when you do. At that point, many grieving people find a support group a good place to find a listening ear.

There is no "correct" way to grieve. The important thing is to recognize your need to grieve—and to trust that time will ease the pain.

This man's letter touched a chord in many people who have lost a spouse. Some sent suggestions for coping with grief or getting on with life. Others simply wrote to share their sympathy.

But they all had one message in common, summed up by a woman in Abingdon, Maryland: "I lost my dear husband after forty-six years of marriage. The pain has been unbearable." Losing a spouse is like losing part of oneself.

Yet life demands that we cope with grief, however unbearable it seems. The woman from Maryland says: "I am coping better now. What helped me was keeping busy and a marvelous book to which I go back again and again—*Living When a Loved One Has Died*, by Earl A. Grollman."

Another woman sends advice gleaned from the sudden death of her forty-five-year-old husband: "Let people help you, even if you feel you do not need their help. They need to alleviate their sorrow also.

"Talk about the person who has died as much as you want to. I discovered this was not easy to do. I wanted to talk about him, but others did not want to listen. I realize it hurt them to hear me refer to him, but I always felt better when I could bring his name into my conversation. After all, he was an important part of my life for over twenty years.

"Don't look any farther ahead than one day at a time. Sure, eventually the future must be faced, but don't dwell on it until you feel you are in shape to make decisions.

"Rabbi Harold Kushner's book *When Bad Things Happen to Good People* was also of great help to me. Although I did not agree with all his ideas, it did put my husband's death in proper perspective, so that eventually, instead of saying, 'Why did this happen to me?,' I was able to ask, 'Why not me?'

"Time does not heal, but it makes the hurt bearable."—M.R., Seminole, Florida

Another woman found comfort in keeping busy with other widows: "I have worked with quite a few women who have lost their husbands, and for them and myself evolved a program of keeping busy and helping others that seems to have been beneficial.

"The program includes daily prayer and chores, plus weekly and monthly fun treats—a show, a luncheon, etc.—as well as either learning a new talent or sharing one you have, such as teaching bridge or Spanish (in my case). This seems to have helped some."—M.F., St. Petersburg, Florida

A word about books: They can be helpful, but don't expect a book to answer all your questions or solve your need to grieve.

Books that answer one person's spiritual or emotional needs may not seem at all relevant to someone else. They may seem to avoid the hard questions or offer answers that seem too easy. Even so, many people find that a book can provide a great deal of comfort in a time of grief.

Grieving people need many sources of comfort and support. Books, friends, activities, and an ability to take one day at a time until the future seems less bleak—all of these contribute to the long process of bringing meaning back into life once death seems to have taken all its joys away.

Healthy Mourning

In the midst of grief, the sorrow seems endless. Yet, in time, the degree and emphasis of grief should ease, and life becomes less colored by loss.

But how will you know when grief is healed? Is there such a thing as a "favorable" end to grief, a recovery or completion of the bereavement process? If so, how will you recognize it when it happens?

Studies of grief show that a healthy mourning process does bring you to a recovery, a point where you find that you have regained lost functions or attitudes. You are able to take an interest in your current life and you are more hopeful about things in general. You also find that you can actually enjoy yourself or take pleasure in your activities again, even though you still may have periods of sadness.

Especially in cases where you have lost a spouse, you may discover that you can adapt to new roles, successfully taking on responsibilities that were unfamiliar before. You also begin to accept yourself as a single person, rather than as part of a couple. Many people find that bereavement brings a chance for personal growth or a chance to try new things.

These can all be signs that you are recovering from your loss. That's not necessarily the same as "returning to normal," since the death of a significant person can change the shape of your life. What was "normal" for you before has changed.

The key to all this is time and what you do with it. Grieving time varies for each person. It's misleading and unfair to put a time limit on grief, your own or someone else's.

Yet somehow our culture seems to have decided that the process of mourning a death should be completed in a year. Often, grieving people find that their friends' sympathy runs short even before a year is up.

I once heard about a woman grieving the death of her husband of thirty years who was told six months after his death that she was simply having a "pity party" if she couldn't "get over" her intense grief in that length of time.

Studies show, however, that grief frequently lasts longer than one year, and that while it may be less intense for many people, they should not necessarily expect a full "recovery" within a year. Some people even say that the second year is harder in some ways, especially if the months immediately after the death have been filled with time-absorbing tasks such as settling the estate.

It is a misunderstanding of how human emotions work—and a dangerous disservice to grieving people—to put a time limit on grief. It's hard enough to come to grips with death. The last thing bereaved people need is to be told how they should feel and when.

Recovery from grief will come, but don't try to rush it.

Some people find it helpful to make a list of priorities, ranging from simple but important things like getting dressed or buying groceries to larger matters like making sense of your financial situation. Don't worry about nonessential items. Things that don't make the list you can worry about later. For instance, if you have children, paying attention to their grief and other emotional needs should take precedence over whatever responsibility you may have in dealing with the feelings of other family members or friends.

Suicide Survival

Q: "My seven-year-old son and I are trying to cope with my husband's suicide ten months ago. Do you know of any 'suicide survivor' support groups in my area we could go to? Or perhaps of a counselor or psychologist who specializes in dealing with this problem?"—L.A., Anaheim Hills, California

A: For every suicide, researchers estimate that there are from six to ten people whose lives are deeply affected by that death.

Because suicide is something most people in our society are uncomfortable talking about, "suicide survivors" face a double whammy. They feel rejected and abandoned by the person who has died and cut off from outsiders as well.

Yet the feelings of guilt, anger, and shame that come crashing down on survivors can make them vulnerable to the same impulses that prompted the suicide of their loved one. Studies of suicide survivors have found that they often suffer from physical and psychological problems, and are more prone to suicide than the general population—a condition that can lead to a chain of suicides among family members or friends.

So it is important that you and your son seek help. The good news is that you are not alone; help is available, and it can come in several forms.

You may want to start by reading *Silent Grief: Living in the Wake of Suicide* (Charles Scribner's Sons, $19.95 in hardback).

The book was written by Christopher Lukas, a television writer and producer who lost his mother, an aunt, uncle, and close friend to suicide, and Henry M. Seiden, a clinical psychologist and psychotherapist.

Books like this one can provide information about suicide as well as insights and advice for survivors. But it is also important for you to find people you can talk to, whether it is a self-help group of other survivors, a support group led by a professional therapist, or individual sessions with a professional. Be aware that there is a difference in self-help groups and professional help.

Initially, you and your son may want to consult with a professional, whether a licensed counselor, a clinical psychologist or a psychiatrist, either in a group setting or individual sessions. Later on, you may find a self-help group of other survivors to be a good way to continue your recovery.

To find suicide survivor groups in your area, start by calling your local mental health association, which should be listed in the telephone directory. Someone there should be able to explain the various kinds of professional help available and may even provide a list of names.

Another way to find help is to check the telephone directory for suicide or crisis hotlines. You can usually find them listed under "S" for suicide, "C" for crisis, or sometimes "H" for hotline. Call and tell them you are a suicide survivor and are looking for a support group or professional help.

In the past few years, many areas of the country have developed regional self-help clearing houses, where callers can get information on all kinds of self-help groups.

If hotline numbers or self-help clearing house numbers are not listed in your local directory, you can try directory assistance. In most parts of the country, telephone operators can provide this information.

Guilt and Grieving

Guilt. It's a simple word, but it complicates our lives—and our deaths as well.

A woman in California has some wise observations on the subject:

"I've noticed that the more guilt I have about a person, the more difficult the grieving is after the person's death.

"It only took me two weeks to get over feeling heavy and sad after my grandmother died. I think that was because she spent a month dying in the hospital, and I went as often as I was allowed, even after she stopped knowing me. I showed her before she died how I felt.

"On the other hand, I felt weighed down by the death of a supervisor at my husband's work. I think it was because I'd known about his cancer and had wanted to thank him for some kindnesses but never did. So when I heard about his death, it was a shock. It stayed with me for about a month."

We humans are social animals. The death of one person inevitably affects the lives of many other people.

Death stops the daily give-and-take that characterizes any human relationship. It rudely reminds us that intentions are meaningless if we never follow through. And who can say he always followed through on every good intention?

The death of someone we know or love inevitably raises questions about our own behavior, even our secret attitudes. Did we uphold our responsibilities as a relative or friend? Did we care enough? Did we say what needed to be said? Did we help ease a person's last days on earth?

Sometimes we overdose on guilt, punishing ourselves far beyond the seriousness of the actions or oversights or emotions we regret. Sometimes, however, the guilt is there for a reason.

There are times when guilt seems to paralyze us for reasons we don't understand—plenty of psychologists and psychiatrists have gotten rich on other people's guilt. But guilt is not all bad.

Like physical pain, it can serve to remind us that something is amiss, that we're not living up to the standards we've set for ourselves.

That's what I find so refreshing about this woman's remarks. She recognized guilt for what it was—a reminder that she failed to follow through on her good intentions. She knew this man was dying, but she waited too long to say thank you.

Of course, she feels badly about that. She also knows she's not the prisoner of that one failure; her experience with her grandmother proves that. And she's clearheaded enough to recognize that nothing dooms her to repeat the failure.

One reason we dread the thought of death is because it so often brings with it reasons for guilt. But that's also a reason for facing up to the fact that we should live our lives and conduct our relationships so that when death does interrupt—as it surely will—we'll have fewer regrets, and a lighter burden of guilt.

Acceptance

The nation watched with awe and admiration in August, 1989, when Major Robin L. Higgins walked into a Pentagon briefing, read an eloquent tribute to her husband, Lieutenant Colonel William R. Higgins, and acknowledged that she presumed he had been killed by his captors in Lebanon.

As a fourteen-year Marine veteran, Major Higgins could be expected to remain calm in times of crises. But even one of her military colleagues said later that when Major Higgins read a draft of the statement to her, it brought tears to her eyes, prompting Major Higgins to say "Kathy, stop crying."

Major Higgins's bravery in the face of such tragic loss was a touching moment. But her composure also illustrated something important about grief and our reactions to loss: For each of us, mourning takes an individual form.

Of course there are common characteristics, especially for

the intense period of grief following a death. But the notion that there is a "normal" pattern of grief can sometimes do more harm than good. What about people who don't fit the "normal" mode? Is something wrong with them?

Studies of grief show that the range of "normal" or "healthy" reactions to losses is much wider than we have thought. The loss that triggers the grieving process could be the death of a family member or friend, or even a physical loss, such as sudden blindness or paralysis.

But the reactions can range from the public composure of Major Higgins to the public tears and wailing exhibited by other mourners at funerals or burials. New studies of bereavement have found that between a quarter to two-thirds of grieving widows and widowers are not greatly distressed.

That kind of reaction doesn't fit the expectations that many of us have for someone who has just lost a spouse. In fact, many therapists have assumed that without this brief, intense period of distress or grief, a mourner is less likely to adjust well in the long run, and later on may be plagued by symptoms of delayed grief. More recent research suggests that plenty of people cope with a death without going through a period of intense and obvious distress.

Another assumption many of us cling to is that grief goes away after a given period of time—and, many people seem to think, the sooner the better. It's common for friends of widows or widowers to worry when they aren't "back in the social whirl" after a year. But it's also common for some widows and widowers, or for people mourning the death of a parent or child, to grieve for several years.

The point is, each mourner is different. Equally important, each death is different. Research is now bearing out what common sense tells us: Some deaths, such as those resulting from traumatic accidents, can be more difficult to deal with than others. Moreover, when people can find some kind of meaning in a death, they are better able to come to terms with it.

To most Americans, the death of Lieutenant Colonel Higgins was an outrageous act of barbarism. But Robin Higgins reminded us that his death came in the line of duty, and that in performing that duty he fulfilled his boyhood wish. He made his family proud of him and, for his widow, that helped give meaning to this death.

When Children Face Death

Childhood should be a time to learn about life. But sometimes it brings brushes with death. What happens to children who contract cancer, face the possibility of death, but survive? As cancer-survival rates rise, that question is taking on more importance.

Most of us, I suspect, would say that the psychological scars would depend on how serious the illness had been.

Not so, says Dr. Gregory Fritz, director of child and family psychiatry at Rhode Island Hospital in Providence and chief investigator for a study of fifty-two survivors of childhood cancer. The study, funded by the William T. Grant Foundation, was published in the October, 1988, issue of the *American Journal of Orthopsychiatry.*

Dr. Fritz and his colleagues, Dr. Judith Williams of Brown University and Dr. Michael Amylon of the Children's Hospital at Stanford University, found that the most important influence on the long-term psychological health of these children was their ability to talk openly to their parents and friends about their disease. Support from a best friend and from other peers also made a difference.

Some examples:

—Nine-year-old Judy, suffering from lymphoma, got visits from a large number of her classmates. She often had friends go along when she visited the hospital for outpatient treatments.

—At ten, Mark lost a leg to cancer. He learned to talk about his disease, and later made presentations about it to his ninth-grade science class and to community groups.

—But Luis, a twelve-year-old leukemia patient, came from a

family that didn't communicate easily. He had trouble talking about his illness, withdrew from his friends, and didn't talk much to his doctors. After he finished his treatment, he became obese and left school at fourteen.

"There are no absolutes," Dr. Fritz says. It's possible to violate any rule and have the children turn out okay, or vice versa. But in general, he says, the quality of communication between parents and a child is the most important predictor of the child's ability to make a healthy psychological adjustment.

Even so, parents of cancer patients will not always find it easy to talk about the disease with their child. They may feel they don't know enough or that they'll say something wrong. Worse, they may not want to face it themselves and think, subconsciously perhaps, that if they ignore it the disease will go away. Or maybe they fear that discussing the disease will put wrong ideas in a child's head.

In fact, children know when they're really sick, and their reactions would probably surprise their parents. Dr. Fritz points out that it is common for children, even small children, to want to protect their parents from bad news.

Children whose parents are reluctant to communicate may feel guilty about the pain their condition is causing their family. That's a cruel burden for a sick child to bear. In the long run, it may be as damaging to the child as the disease itself.

Not all parents will need help in deciding how to talk with their children. But for those who do, every hospital should have support staff available to help them. If not, families "should raise hell about it," Dr. Fritz says. "That's standard of care."

Good communication helps parents as well as children, and parents need to worry about their psychological scars, too. "I believe that two or more years after treatment, kids generally have less trouble with their illness than their parents, in terms of worrying about it on a day-to-day basis," Dr. Fritz says.

"What is most remarkable to me is the capacity of the human spirit to grow and survive in the face of overwhelming obstacles," he adds. "Most kids do this pretty well."

The fact that researchers are now conducting psychological studies of children who have survived life-threatening diseases is an encouraging sign of the progress that is being made in many areas of medical technology. But what about the cases in which the outcome is not so good?

The death of a child is always devastating, regardless of the age of the child or how the death occurred.

Just as every child is unique, the circumstances surrounding each parent's grief are different. But that doesn't make some losses easier to take than others. Our society seems to inject an element of competition into just about every aspect of life. We don't need competitive grief.

A parent in Florida writes: "Our two-and-a-half-year-old daughter died in recovery from complications resulting from surgery to correct a serious congenital heart disease. . . . I disagree that people whose children die suddenly have a greater grief than parents with children who have been ill for some time.

"Several books I have read indicate that the death of an ill child, whether it be heart problems, cancer, etc., should have been prepared for.

"If we started preparing the minute we were told our child was ill, we would have given up the long, hard fight that we had to teach our child. Then, indeed, you better be prepared—prepared for the guilt that would soon follow because you were too busy preparing instead of fighting. There is not time to prepare, or to say goodbye."

For a parent, the circumstances of a death don't change the emotional devastation. The death of a child puts a parent "so far into major emotional pain that you've already blown the circuits," as the physician and author Dr. Robert Buckman puts it. Trying to decide which circumstance would make grief easier is "a bit like asking whether you'd rather be strangled or shot."

But in arguing that a parent cannot "prepare" for the death of a child, this parent may be overlooking the strength of the human spirit. It's true that you can't, like a good Boy Scout, "be prepared" for the death of your child, at least not in any ordinary sense of the word "prepared." But if you know the child is likely to die, you can take steps to reduce the damage—in the same sense that if you see a tornado coming, you would move away from the windows.

One way to "prepare" is to discuss your fears—with your spouse, with the doctor, and perhaps even with your child, especially if the child indicates a desire to talk. No one likes to think about dying, but that doesn't stop people from making wills. And making a will doesn't indicate that a person is giving up all interest in life.

Physicians who work with terminally ill people testify to the remarkable ability of their patients to fight for the best outcome even while preparing, in emotional, spiritual, and practical terms, for the worst.

In judging when or whether to discuss the possibility of death with a very sick child, it's good to remember that children, like adults, know when their bodies are failing them.

They also know how much their condition is hurting their parents and other people they love, and that can make them feel guilty. This was graphically illustrated in the book and television movie "Go Toward the Light," when a young boy suffering from AIDS asked his grandmother whether she and his parents would be "mad at him" if he died.

Dying people, whatever their age, have enough to contend with. They don't need the isolation that can come from the fear of honest communication. If they want to talk frankly, then people they love should be willing to listen.

Long Odds Don't Make a Child Less Special

Expressing condolences can be a tricky matter. So often the words we say to people sound very different to them than the thoughts we are trying to express.

Different situations can evoke different sentiments—and

hold different kinds of pitfalls for well-meaning friends. A mother in California has some practical advice for one of those special situations, the death of a young child who was born with multiple birth defects.

We all know that for many of these children survival is a battle against the odds. But long odds don't make a child less unique or special. And, despite what others may think the people who love that child should rationally "expect," the child's handicaps don't make his death any less painful for them.

Here are some wise words from Lorna Bateham of Orange, California, who has lived through such a loss:

"In December 1988, we lost our beloved son Eric. Eric was two years old and suffered from multiple birth defects. He died suddenly and unexpectedly from a seizure in the wee hours of the morning.

"After his death we heard many well-meaning comments from friends and family, such as: 'It was God's will,' or 'Don't you think it's for the best since he was so handicapped?' and even 'You knew he wouldn't live a long time. Weren't you expecting this?'

"While we realize people may not know what to say in a situation such as ours and that these words were offered as a source of comfort, we have some suggestions that would truly offer words of comfort and let the parents and family of the child know that other people thought he was special, too, and will be remembered not for the handicaps he had but for the unique, wonderful little boy he truly was.

"1. Talk about what made the child special. For Eric it was the big smile he gave everyone he met, from doctors with needles to his big brothers.

"2. Talk about the quality of life the child had. Acknowledge that he was a beloved member of the family.

"3. Tell the family he'll be missed by you as you know they will miss him.

"4. Offer to be there to listen to the family in a nonjudgmental way. They have suffered a devastating loss in no way diminished because the child was handicapped.

"5. In the days and months following the funeral share memories of the child with the family so they will know he is not forgotten."

Handicaps don't lessen the bonds of love a person is capable of forming. Neither do they make death easier for loved ones to take. If we judged losses by the perfection—physical, mental, or spiritual—of the deceased, who among us could expect any sympathy at all?

Grief is a universal emotion. But each experience of grief is different, just as the person we mourn was different from all other people. In living with grief each of us finds different answers to its pain. Here is one story from a mother who found that "getting on with it" didn't mean she had to forget her daughter. As this woman learned, there may not be a "cure" for grief, but there are ways to live with it:

"On Easter Sunday, 1975, our beautiful seventeen-year-old daughter, Niecy, was thrown from her horse.

"That day began the trauma that would last the rest of my life. Niecy suffered a severe brain concussion. She was in a coma for thirty days. When she woke she was blind and paralyzed. She could speak but she didn't make sense. She did, however, recognize our voices and would call out, "Hi, Mom. Hi, Dad," whenever we entered the room.

"In spite of a team of excellent doctors, on June 3, Niecy died. She didn't die in quiet slumber, nor holding my hand, as in the movies. She died in ugly convulsions that wracked her frail little body . . . I never realized that children died—until mine did.

"Thirteen years later my heart is still breaking. Time has not healed this wound. Neither has reading countless books on the subject, everything from Elizabeth Kubler Ross to Robert Schuller. I attended group therapy and one-on-one counseling. I went to movies, plays, and talked with others who had lost a loved one. The results were the same, my heart was still breaking.

"About a year ago I came to grips with the fact that my heart was not going to mend because I couldn't. If I were to move ahead in my life, I would have to do so with my brokenness still there.

"Once I accepted this fact and stopped trying to be okay when I wasn't, I was able to move forward. The special sparkle I had lost was replaced by a tremendous empathy for people. I became a good listener. I could recognize instinctively other broken hearts. I was able to understand their pain, though their experience itself was not my own.

"From the day we are born we experience some measure of grief. Parents grieve when their children grow up and leave home. We grieve for lost love, lost memories, lost opportunities, lost dreams, lost friends, and lost puppies. But we never talk about it.

"People never talked to me about Niecy. They talked to me about getting on with my life. And when I failed to 'get on with it' I felt terribly guilty. I wanted to talk about Niecy. I wanted to talk about her life, not her death. She was a fantastic human being, a lover of animals, a poet, a child so akin to nature as to be part creature herself.

"When I attend a group the focus is on death and how to deal with it. I wanted to focus on the one who had died.

"I wanted to say: 'I'm broken, stop trying to fix me!' because it's okay, and I'm okay. There will never be another Niecy, but there was once, and I'm a better person for having experienced this remarkable person. Niecy is a gift of life even in death. I couldn't face life without her, and at long last I realize I don't have to.

"The power of life is love and death cannot take that from us."—J.V., Clewiston, Florida

The Compassionate Friends

We expect parents to die before children. But when children precede their parents in death, the loss seems more unjust and harder to bear.

Nothing can change what we often perceive as the injustice of death. Yet as many grieving parents have learned, coming to terms with the death of a child can be easier when it is not done alone.

That is the purpose of The Compassionate Friends, a national network of support groups for families who have lost a child. The Compassionate Friends, generally known as TCF (the "T" is included to distinguish it from the Cystic Fibrosis organization), grew out of a British clergyman's experience as a hospital chaplain in the 1960s.

When Simon Stephen, a young Anglican priest, took up his post as assistant chaplain at a hospital in Coventry, England, he was distressed by the treatment given parents who had lost a child. They were simply handed their child's belongings in a paper bag, asked to sign the necessary papers, and sent away to cope as best they could.

One day, however, when two young boys died in the same room, Rev. Stephen simply pulled back the curtains and let the two families grieve together. Later the families asked him to form a discussion group for bereaved parents.

The idea spread to the United States in 1971, and since then has grown into a network of about six hundred chapters throughout the country. By 1977, TCF had a national board of directors and a national headquarters based in Oak Brook, Ill.

The primary focus for TCF chapters is on parents and siblings, but the groups also provide help for grieving grandparents. Chapters are generally autonomous, with the national headquarters providing guidance and a link to other groups.

The groups are based on seven general principles:

1. TCF offers friendship and understanding to bereaved parents.

2. TCF believes that bereaved parents can help each other toward a positive resolution of their grief.

3. TCF reaches out to all bereaved parents across artificial barriers of religion, race, economic class, or ethnic group.

4. TCF understands that every bereaved parent has individual needs and rights.

5. TCF helps bereaved parents primarily through local chapters.

6. TCF chapters belong to their members.

7. TCF chapters are coordinated nationally to extend help to each other and to individual bereaved parents everywhere.

For more information about TCF groups in your area, contact The Compassionate Friends, P.O. Box 3696, Oak Brook, Ill. 60522. Telephone: (312) 990-0010.

Chapter **6**

Taken by Surprise?

The problem with death—at least, *one* of the problems with death—is that it almost always surprises us, no matter how much we may think we expect it and are prepared. If nothing else, we're often caught off guard by our reaction to the awesome finality of death.

Death itself is such an overwhelming experience that we seldom think beyond that event to what comes next—what the survivors are left to cope with.

Death at Home

Here is a question from a woman in San Diego about some practical matters we all need to consider:

Q: "What steps must be followed when there is a death in the family at home? Do you have to call the police, and do they contact the coroner's office, or do you have to have someone do this for you? Does the coroner have to come to your residence and if you haven't made advance funeral planning, do you have to wait until he tells you to contact the funeral director?"

A: Exact procedures vary from state to state. In general, however, deaths at home fall into two categories—expected or sudden. In either case, the cause of death must be determined before a funeral director can remove the body.

If the person has been ill and under the care of a doctor, your first call could be to the attending physician who can certify the cause of death. In these cases, it may be possible for the doctor to notify the funeral director directly. If a member of your family is suffering from a terminal illness and intends to die at home, it would be a good idea to ask your physician beforehand what procedure you should follow.

If the death was not anticipated, but the person had been

recently under a doctor's care (generally, within the past year), you may want to inquire whether the physician would be willing to come to the house and determine the cause of death.

In most cases, however, your first call would go to your local emergency number or to the police, if only to make sure that nothing can be done to revive the person. Paramedic teams and police usually work together in these cases. Both departments will respond to a call reporting a death.

Once the fact of death has been established, the police will contact the medical examiner or coroner in order to determine an official cause of death. Procedures for this vary according to state laws, and in some states the process may even differ from county to county.

One reason for an investigation is to determine whether there is anything suspicious about the death that may require criminal prosecution. But medical examiners often say that a more common aspect of their work is simply to try to provide answers to the questions of anguished families struggling to understand what has happened and why.

Once medical examiners or coroners determine the cause of death, they can release the body to a funeral director. If they are not certain about the cause of death, they may order an autopsy to be performed first.

People who plan cremation should be aware that in some states a medical examiner's release is required before a body can be cremated. This simply certifies that there are no lingering questions about the cause of death.

In any state, it is a good idea to check with your local officials on the exact procedure your family should follow in case of a sudden death and to have phone numbers handy for emergency services, the police, and your family physician.

Death Away from Home

What about death away from home? In most cases, the procedure would be similar—your first calls should probably go to
emergency services or to the police, in case something can be
done to revive the person. Then, unless it is evident, a medical
examiner or coroner will need to determine the cause of death.
Officials may need to make calls to the family physician or other
people familiar with the person's medical records.

Once the cause of death is established, you will need to make
plans for disposition of the body (see next chapter). If you want
to return the body home for burial, your best bet would be to
contact a funeral director in your hometown, who can be helpful in cutting through the red tape involved in transporting the
body, especially if it involves crossing state lines or the use of
public transportation.

When death occurs abroad, however, things get a bit more
complicated.

According to the U.S. State Department, each year about six
thousand Americans die abroad. Many of them are residents of
foreign countries, but in about two thousand cases death comes
unexpectedly to a traveler. For the family, the suddenness of
death is compounded by more red tape and expense, and a
demand for even faster decisions about disposition of the body,
than for a death closer to home. It's a time when families who
failed to plan for death can find themselves wishing they knew
exactly how their relative felt about things like cremation or
burial in a foreign country.

Consider these State Department estimates of the approxi-
mate cost, as of March 1989, of preparing and returning human
remains or ashes by air freight to the East Coast:

From London: $1,800 for the return of remains; $500 for
ashes.

From Bern: $5,500 for remains; $2,000 for cremation and
return of ashes.

From Nairobi: $1,800 for remains; $933 for ashes.

From Tokyo: $6,870 for remains; $3,187 for ashes.

From Acapulco: $2,200–$2,500 for remains; $1,300 for ashes.

From Tel Aviv: $1,550 for remains. (Cremation is not available. There is also an extra charge for embalming, which may range from $650 to $1,500.)

U.S. embassies and consulates around the world routinely assist American citizens when emergencies come up, and death is no exception. When an American dies abroad, consular officials provide "a report of death" to accompany the local country's death certificate. This State Department document can be used for legal purposes in the United States.

For deceased Americans who were traveling alone, the State Department takes on a more active role, beginning with notification of the next of kin. These are the tough cases because decisions about the body must be made immediately. In some parts of the world, for example, there are inadequate morgue facilities, and a body not disposed of in a short period of time will automatically be cremated or buried according to local customs.

The State Department has no funds to pay for cremation or preparation for burial, and if the family wishes for the remains or ashes to be returned to this country, they must forward the payment, sometimes within as short a period as twenty-four hours. Scan those estimates again, and you can see why it is important to know how both you and a loved one feel about cremation or where and how you are buried. The State Department cannot make these decisions on behalf of families.

Surely there are travelers who are foresighted and organized enough to carry with them exact instructions in case of sudden death, but if you're like me, you probably don't know many of them. Still, there is one step everyone should take—and one that many people neglect—that could help enormously in this situation. That is simply to fill out completely the "Emergency Contact" section of the passport application. It is also a good idea to check your medical insurance to see whether it provides coverage abroad, medical evacuation in case you need

further treatment, and the return of remains or ashes. Beyond
that, any discussion of plans or preferences with your next of
kin will help make their decisions easier.

The vast majority of Americans who travel abroad return
home alive and well, probably complaining about flight delays
or airline food or the long lines at customs. Sometimes, however,
death sneaks up on us in strange and foreign places, making the
familiar hassles of traveling seem small indeed. That's when it
pays—emotionally and even financially—to have thought ahead
about how much it matters where and how our mortal remains
are returned to the earth.

Transporting a Body

A woman writes:

"My eighty-eight-year-old grandmother recently has become obsessed with dying. Not in a morbid way, but merely
recognizing that at her age, 'You have to get things ready.'
Recently she asked me to find a lawyer to draft what now—after
three previous documents—is going to be, she promises, her
last, her very last, will and testament. It wasn't a difficult job.
She knew precisely what she wanted. Every pearl necklace had
been accounted for, every piece of furniture and each photograph. She seemed to have thought of everything, until the
lawyer asked how she wanted her body to be sent from Baltimore, where she lives now, to New York, where she is going to
be buried.

"She stared at him blankly. Sensing her total lack of understanding of her options, he laid out a couple. She could be sent by
air or by rail.

"She sat silent for a moment, her mouth open and her eyes
wide, clearly baffled by the whole thing. Then she snapped at
him and at me: 'What do I care? I'll be dead. Do whatever you
want.'

"The problem is I have no idea what to do. My only experience in shipping things other than luggage by air was sending my dog in a travel case, and he didn't like it much. Is there a special place for coffins? Also, do the airlines put the coffins right in there with the suitcases?

"The train is even more confusing. Do you book a special freight train or just use Amtrak?

"Also, who takes care of the coffin? Do I have to ride along on the train or the plane?"—L.C., Baltimore

A: There are several options for transporting her body. The three most common are commercial airlines, private air transport companies, or door-to-door service provided by a funeral home in a hearse or specially equipped station wagon. Transportation by train is also possible, but it is less common nowadays.

Your best bet would be to call some funeral homes in Baltimore and explain your situation briefly. Ask for an appointment; a face-to-face meeting will help you choose someone you are comfortable with. Funeral directors should be able to give you estimates for at least the three most common ways of transporting the body. Several factors will go into the estimate, such as the distance by highway (fees for a private hearse or station wagon are usually based on mileage), the proximity of airports and the cost of the outer shipping container that airlines require to protect caskets. (Yes, caskets are shipped along with regular luggage; no escort is necessary, but family members who do want to accompany the body sit in the passenger compartment.)

Be as specific as you can with the funeral director; you may even suggest a route that a hearse could take. That will help with the mileage estimate.

Funeral directors provide an essential service, and they deal with these matters every day. A big part of their job is spending time with people like you who are planning ahead. Remember that as a potential customer, you are under no obligation for the information they provide. As in any other business transaction, you should gather as much information about prices and other factors as you need in order to make a decision you can be comfortable with.

Your time will be well spent. Regardless of the method of transportation you choose, you will need the services of a funeral home in Baltimore. Assuming your grandmother dies there, her body will need to be embalmed or placed in a hermetically sealed casket or airtight container before being transported to New York. Even in states where the law does not require these safeguards, the laws of nature do.

Organ and Tissue Donations

When a family member dies, decisions have to be made quickly. One of the most important is the decision to allow parts of the body to be donated. Many people carry donor cards, or check the donor option on their driver's license. But the fact is that hospitals will not retrieve organs or tissues if the next-of-kin objects. That's why it's a good idea to discuss these decisions as a family.

One of the difficult aspects about donating major organs such as hearts, lungs, or livers is that these organs usually come from young, healthy people who have died suddenly. In order to preserve the organs, the donors, although technically dead, are kept on breathing machines. That means that families who have been struck with tragedy are asked for permission to remove vital organs from a person who appears to them merely to be in a coma rather than truly dead. For those who have not thought about the issue beforehand and who have not made a commitment to donate organs or tissues, the decision can be emotionally wrenching.

But the reward can be great. Donations are literally a gift of life. They can also enhance lives in important ways.

At twenty-five, Robert Pierce of Bowie, Maryland, is learning to walk again. Thanks to medical technology—and to a tissue donor—he can look forward to a normal life, despite the fact that surgeons had to remove a tumor and four inches from his thighbone.

A few years ago, Mr. Pierce would almost certainly have lost his leg to amputation. And until recently, the only other option would have been a metal replacement of the lower thigh and knee, a much riskier and more complicated procedure. Instead, Mr. Pierce received a bone transplant using tissue from a cadaver.

We hear a lot about the miracles of modern transplantation techniques. But those "miracles" could become commonplace. Many transplant operations are now routine and make more sense economically than other forms of treatment.

For instance, many specialists believe that at least half of the thirty thousand people who begin kidney dialysis each year could have successful transplants instead. But doctors transplant only about nine thousand kidneys a year.

That leaves six thousand people who could benefit from transplants but never get them. Data from the Health Care Financing Administration shows that taxpayers would also benefit from the transplants—saving $200 million annually.

Each year, more than two million people die in the United States. But fewer than fifty thousand of them become organ or tissue donors.

In some cases, next-of-kin turn down requests of hospital personnel to retrieve tissues or organs. Often, however, families are never asked about donation. Yet families rarely deny requests when the deceased has indicated a willingness to donate organs or tissues, through a universal donor card, a check-off on a driver's license or, best of all, prior discussion of the subject with the family.

Anne Madden, director of transplantation services for the National Capital Chapter of the American Red Cross, stresses that no card can guarantee that you will become a donor. Even if you have a universal donor card or other documents stating your wishes, hospital personnel will not retrieve organs or tissues from your body if your family objects. That's why it helps to discuss the matter beforehand.

That may seem awkward, but it's really no more awkward than making a will.

Organs—the kidney, liver, heart, lungs, and pancreas—can save lives. Corneas can restore eyesight. Middle ear tissue can enable people to hear. Connective tissue can help in throat, abdominal, orthopedic, plastic, and oral surgery. Thin strips of skin can save the lives of burn victims. Bones can help people like Robert Pierce walk again.

None of this interferes with the rituals of burial. Organ and tissue donors can still have open-casket funerals, if their families wish.

For more information about becoming a tissue donor, call the American Red Cross at 1-800-2TISSUE. Information about donation of organs is available from the American Council on Transplantation at (703) 836-4301.

The Living Will

Advances in medical technology have added another item to the list of important mortal matters—the living will. A living will is a document stating which kinds of treatment you want to be withheld or used if you become terminally ill or permanently unconscious.

Most states now have living will legislation, and your document should be drawn up according to the laws of your own state. However, in those states without such legislation, courts of law generally have recognized a person's right to refuse medical treatment, and a living will is considered the best way of specifying your intentions. It is not necessary for your state to have a living will law for you to spell out your wishes in advance.

The Society for the Right to Die can provide a generic living will, suitable for use in states without living will laws. It also provides forms that follow the specific laws of other states. The forms and an accompanying list of guidelines are free, although the society welcomes a tax-deductible contribution. Write to: Society for the Right to Die, Box A, 250 W. 57th St., New York, N.Y. 10107.

Living wills play an important role in helping people retain some control over their medical treatment in cases where they are no longer able to make decisions. In many cases, the fact that a patient has taken the time to sign a living will is a great relief to the family. It spares them the burden of making such a big decision.

However, it is important to know that living wills are some times overruled—especially in cases where the family is not comfortable with a decision to remove or withhold life-prolonging treatment. That's why it's always a good idea to discuss your wishes with your family.

Aside from living wills many states allow people to appoint a proxy or agent who has legal authority to make decisions about medical care, including the decision to withhold or terminate treatment. Even if you choose this option, it's a good idea to inform your family of your wishes. When more people understand your intentions, you are less likely to encounter hesitation on the part of the hospital in carrying them out.

You certainly should discuss the matter with your physician, and a copy of your living will should be made part of your medical records. Other copies should be given to your next-of-kin and to your proxy or agent. You should keep your own copy with your important personal papers, but it should be easy for someone else to get to in case of an emergency. Don't hide it away in a safe deposit box.

Laws and procedures can vary from state to state, reflecting varying attitudes toward death in different parts of this diverse country. For that reason, if you regularly spend time in two or more states—say, summers in Michigan and winters in Florida— you would be wise to sign living wills in each state.

The courts have generally recognized that people should have the right to refuse medical treatment and that living wills are a valid way of expressing their intentions. And because the legal system is putting more importance on these documents, *not* having one can be taken as a signal that you *do* want every medical measure available, no matter how hopeless your situation. When we are offered a choice in an important matter, as living will legislation does, we run the risk of paying a penalty for not bothering to exercise that choice.

Chapter 7

Deaths and Dispositions

When a death occurs, one person's worldly cares come to an end. But for survivors, the choices are just beginning. Those choices begin with decisions about the "final disposition" of the remains—decisions that must be made quickly. Here are some common questions about choices and procedures:

Q: "Recently I did some reading about funeral planning, and I ran across the term 'final disposition' in reference to bodies of the deceased. I assume this refers to burial. If so, why don't people just use that word? Is this part of the bad habit of trying to sanitize death?"

A: In many parts of the world, burial is the most common form of final disposition. But it is not the only form.

Many bodies are entombed, or placed in above-ground mausoleums. The procedures are similar to an earth burial, since the body is placed in a casket and is usually driven from the funeral ceremony to the cemetery in a procession.

Entombment is the traditional form of final disposition in some areas. In New Orleans, for example, high water tables make ground burial impossible, and the rows of mausoleums in cemeteries give them the look of "cities of the dead."

In places where ground burial is possible, elaborate mausoleums serve chiefly as a statement of the wealth or status of a family, or perhaps of the respect or rank a person earned in life.

Cremation is another form of final disposition that is gaining increasing acceptance in North America. However, this option is still not as popular here as in many parts of the world. The cremation rate is roughly 15 percent in the United States, and about 25 percent in Canada. By contrast, in European countries more than half of those who die are cremated. In some cultures, such as Japan, cremation is the most common form of final disposition of a body.

The use of the term final disposition instead of a specific

word like burial reflects the fact that there are several choices in determining what to do when someone dies. You're right, however, that the terminology surrounding death and disposition of the dead is often filled with euphemisms that attempt to take away the sting of reality—and "final disposition" sounds suspiciously abstract and impersonal.

But look at the term again. "Final" indicates permanence. That body will never again be a living, breathing person. Yet because it was once a human being, there must be a proper, dignified disposition of the remains.

Funeral directors say that the committal, the point when a body reaches its final resting place, is often the most powerful part of the funeral ceremonies. This is the time when mourners actually give up the remains, the moment that most symbolizes the fact that death results in permanent separation.

Many families find comfort in having a specific place to visit in remembering a loved one. Others may not feel a strong attachment to a particular plot of land, and may prefer instead to cremate a loved one and scatter the ashes in some special place.

These are deeply personal attitudes. If you have strong feelings or even mild preferences in the disposition of your own remains, you should make those known to your family or friends.

Burial Versus Cremation

Q: "My mother and I have been talking of dying and burial as opposed to cremation. We got quite graphic about what happens to the body after burial. We don't know whom to ask about such questions and we hoped you could help:

"1. After embalming and burial, doesn't the body decompose and become a feeding ground for bacteria, etc.? Wouldn't it be cleaner and neater to be cremated? Do the ashes become a feeding ground for those 'things'?

"2. After the viewing is over, does the body get cremated in the coffin that was chosen by the family (usually quite expensive) or is it removed to a box that burns? If so, what happens to the expensive coffin?

"I am just trying to decide which I prefer, cremation or burial."

A: It's certainly natural to wonder what happens to our bodies after death. Embalming does not preserve a body forever, and you should be aware that it is rarely necessary. But it does accomplish its primary purpose—to slow down the decay process. This gives families more flexibility in scheduling funeral services, although some funeral homes are equipped with body coolers that serve the same purpose. Embalming can also be important to some families if the body is to be viewed by the public; it is much easier to use cosmetics effectively on embalmed bodies.

After burial, even embalmed bodies become the target of the "things" you refer to. But the exact rate of decay will depend on any number of factors, such as the temperature and humidity inside the grave. Decay may seem messy but it is a natural process; it happens to all living tissue once life is over.

In that sense, cremation may seem "cleaner and neater" to you. The ashes that are left—essentially lime and calcium from the bones—have been subjected to such high temperatures that they are sterile. They contain nothing for bacteria to feed on.

From your second question I assume that you would prefer a viewing and a traditional service, even if you choose to be cremated. Bodies are usually placed in some kind of container for cremation. Many people who want to be cremated after a traditional service prefer an inexpensive pressed-wood coffin covered with a flannel or felt material, usually gray. These are not showy coffins, but they are dignified and appropriate.

Some funeral homes will rent a casket, essentially a shell into which a "cocoon" holding the body can be inserted. After the service, the cocoon and body are removed and cremated. However, in some cases renting a casket can cost more than buying a cloth-covered one.

You can be cremated in a more expensive wooden or metal casket. But these coffins are more difficult to burn and some crematoriums charge extra, sometimes as much as double the regular fee.

Metal caskets are almost impossible to burn. During cremation paint peels off the outside and the interior is destroyed, but generally the bulk of the coffin remains intact. I wouldn't advise using a metal casket for cremation, unless you don't trust the funeral home or crematorium and want to make absolutely certain the casket will never be used again.

If you want to purchase an expensive casket but do not want to be cremated in it, here's an idea you might want to consider. Many funeral homes do charity work, and some people who have chosen cremation have arranged to buy a casket for the viewing and service and then donate it to the funeral home for use later in a charity or hardship case. You would need to discuss this idea beforehand with funeral directors in your area.

Embalming

A mother writes: "Almost two years ago, my fourteen-year-old daughter died in her sleep. Although she always seemed to be in excellent health, it was discovered in the autopsy that she had a rare heart disorder that caused her sudden death. After her death and burial, I realized how very little I (and most other people) know about the embalming procedure. Exactly what happens to the body from the time it's picked up until you see it in the funeral home? Her teenaged friends and even our ten-year-old daughter had so many questions regarding this, and I wasn't able to answer them."

A: The embalming process essentially involves replacing the blood and other bodily fluids with a preservative such as formaldehyde. Embalming is rarely required by law. But families that intend to have a public viewing of the body usually choose to have it done, since embalming's preservative powers give them more leeway in scheduling a funeral service.

When a body arrives at the funeral home, it is taken into a preparation room where it is placed on a slanted embalming table. The body is washed, the eyes are closed and the mouth, nose, and other openings are sealed.

In the embalming process, blood is drained through a vein, and the embalming fluid is injected into an artery. A machine is almost always used for this procedure.

Two cavities in the torso—the pleural cavity (where the lungs are located) and the abdominal area—are also flushed out and replaced by a "cavity treatment" embalming fluid. For this, the embalmer usually makes use of a hydro-aspirator, a hand-held device which produces a spray of water as well as a suction.

The embalming fluids gradually seep into the tissue, changing the body's protein into a gel. To prevent the fluid from leaking from the body, openings in the body, even nicks on the skin, or spots where needles were injected, are sealed. Nostrils are packed with cotton, and the mouth is usually sewn shut with a single stitch.

Embalmers are adept at restoring natural features to bodies that have been injured or to people who die after a long illness, and they have a range of techniques to deal with various difficulties. They can replace missing hair, rebuild fractured features or disguise the effects of the drastic weight loss that accompanies a long, wasting illness.

Before it is placed in the casket, the body is dressed and prepared for viewing. Fingernails are cleaned, hair is shampooed and set, and men get a shave. Funeral directors usually encourage families to bring in a recent photograph of the deceased to guide them in applying cosmetics. The families often furnish the clothing to be used and, for women, they may also bring in eye shadow, lipstick or other makeup.

The entire process can take up to several hours, depending largely on the amount of restorative or cosmetic work that must be done to give the body a natural look.

Many funeral directors say the goal of embalming is to give family and friends a last image of their loved one, which allows them a chance to say goodbye.

You should know that except in rare cases, embalming is not required by law. Some people oppose embalming on religious grounds, and it is quite possible to have a viewing of the body without having it embalmed. It is also possible to ship an unembalmed body to another location, using dry ice, and a hermetically sealed casket.

If this is your preference, check your area for a funeral home that is equipped with body coolers, which effectively retard the decaying process long enough to allow for a viewing and a funeral service. The funeral directors' association in your state should be able to give you a list of such establishments.

Grave Sites

A man in rural Maryland asks: "Why can't I be buried in my own backyard?"

The answer seems to be that you can. In many parts of the country there are no regulations that would stop you.

There are no federal laws governing burial procedures, although many states have cemetery regulatory boards that might oversee such requests. But anyone considering burial on family land should check first with local zoning and health authorities, a suggestion that would be valid in any state.

Regardless of the law, using your yard for burial would probably not be practical. As American society has grown more mobile, few families can count on spending more than one generation in the same house. Real estate agents warn that turning part of the yard into a burial area would make your property more difficult to sell, even if you have a lot spacious enough to accommodate a grave. In financial terms you would probably end up losing more money in the resale value of your house and land than you save by not having to purchase a cemetery lot.

Even if you dream of keeping your house and land in the family for years to come, you should think carefully before establishing a burial plot. Your children might agree with your vision of a family burial ground, but will their children and grandchildren be willing—and able—to maintain the property?

You may in fact be putting your descendants in the awkward position of having to move your grave to a more traditional setting. Even in terms of maintaining the grave you will be creating extra work for them.

Robert M. Fells, general counsel to the American Cemetery Association, points out that maintenance and groundskeeping is a major expense for cemeteries. Just think about the work it takes to keep the grass trimmed around all those headstones and crypts and you get some idea of the time and effort involved.

That—and the fact that we humans like to think that our graves will be reasonably permanent—accounts for the fact that almost every state requires cemeteries to set aside an endowment to ensure that the term "perpetual care" really does have some meaning. Generally, states require that a minimum of 10 percent of the price of a cemetery lot be set aside for future maintenance, but some states require more, and many cemeteries voluntarily exceed that amount. When you look at cemetery lots, it's a good idea to ask how much of your cost is set aside for future maintenance.

If you still have your heart set on a burial spot on your own land, you would be wise to make provisions for future maintenance by following the procedures required of a regular cemetery. That would include an endowment fund for maintenance and clear instructions specifying who is to administer the fund and oversee the burial area.

When we think of graves, we think of permanence. But anyone who has driven down a country road and encountered a deserted, dilapidated church, with its equally neglected graveyard, knows that time can undo the best intentions of any generation.

Traditions and Trends

Funeral practices—and funeral spending—depend on social trends and shared cultural assumptions. But American society has been through dramatic changes in recent years, and some of them directly affect the attitudes on which the funeral industry is built.

Cremation statistics are significant. In 1987, the cremation rate surpassed 15 percent; doubling the rate recorded ten years earlier.

Many areas of the country have businesses, often known as cremation societies which offer a direct service to the public, allowing families to bypass funeral homes altogether. (Unlike voluntary groups affiliated with the Continental Association of Funeral and Memorial Societies, these "societies" are profit-making organizations).

The societies offer cremation for a few hundred dollars. This alternative is known as "direct cremation," since the body is taken directly from the place of death to the crematory. A family member must verify the identity of the body at the crematory, but there is neither a laying-out of the body nor a formal viewing for family and friends.

Not all cremations bypass funeral homes, however. As cremation gains acceptance in this country, funeral homes are making an effort to incorporate the trend into their business. Many families choose cremation along with the other components of a traditional American funeral, including embalming and viewing of the body, then a funeral service after which the body is cremated.

Funeral homes now offer a range of urns to contain the ashes—at a range of prices. (Ashes are usually returned to the family in a small cardboard box.)

So far, cremation is largely an urban phenomenon. It is also a sign of a more mobile society, one in which geographical roots are becoming less important and in which calling together families is an increasingly complicated procedure. Many families are finding it easier to plan a memorial service, at which the body is not present, than a traditional funeral, at which the body is always present and which must take place within a few days of the death.

Not surprisingly, in some Western states the percentage of bodies cremated rather than buried exceeds 30 percent, more than double the national rate. In the East, Florida has an exceptionally high cremation rate (31 percent).

Even so, the United States has a long way to go before it catches up with other Western nations. The cremation rate in Great Britain is 67 percent. Next door, Canada also exceeds the United States, with a cremation rate of 25 percent.

As cremation gains in popularity, some odd dilemmas crop up. A few years ago, funeral directors in Florida realized they had a delicate problem on their hands. Their storage rooms were filling up with containers of unclaimed cremated remains, some of which had been there more than half a century.

In some cases the deceased had no immediate survivors and had left no directions beyond a request for cremation. Sometimes the widows or widowers had planned to claim the remains within a few weeks, but died themselves before doing so.

Then, too, there were plenty of instances in which survivors apparently didn't understand that while cremation satisfies the law's demand for the "final disposition" of a body, the ashes that emerge from the fire are the tangible remains of a human life and call for something more dignified that being dumped into the trash bin.

Jim Wylie, executive director of the Florida Funeral Directors Association, estimates that sixteen thousand containers of ashes were left unclaimed in 1986 alone—about 40 percent of all cremations that took place in Florida that year. Cremation is more popular in Florida than in many other parts of the country, largely because the state has a large population of retirees, many of whom have cut ties to their former homes and aren't particularly sentimental about being buried in the places where they've built a new life.

In 1987 the Florida legislature stepped in, passing a law that allows funeral homes to dispose of remains that are still unclaimed after a 120-day waiting period. In 1988, the law became retroactive, covering the thousands of remains stored for years in funeral homes around the state.

Even so, funeral directors are understandably reluctant to make decisions that survivors might challenge in future years. Some can cite instances in which a family returned to the funeral home after another death, recalled the long-forgotten ashes of a family member, and eagerly claimed them.

For that reason, many Florida funeral directors are careful to say they will not "discard" remains, but will simply use the law as permission to dispose of them in some way they consider appropriate—perhaps burying them together with other ashes in a special plot or having them scattered at sea. Then they can tell any family members who might inquire later that the ashes were treated in an appropriate and dignified manner.

Besides giving funeral homes a legal way out of an awkward problem, the law is also making families aware of their responsibility to plan for disposal of the ashes. And for people who decide beforehand that they want their bodies to be cremated—especially for those who may end up with no immediate survivors—the law is a reminder that in their request for cremation they should specify what they want done with their ashes.

There are many possibilities. One is to place the ashes in a niche at a columbarium, the name given to buildings designed for that purpose. Many cemeteries have such facilities. In some parts of the country, churches have installed columbariums which, in essence, become the modern version of the old churchyard cemetery. Some cemeteries will allow burial of ashes in a family plot, marked with a memorial stone. Other cemeteries have scatter gardens or a lake designated for the purpose.

In coastal areas, families often like to take the ashes of a loved one out to sea or onto a lake to scatter them. Other people prefer a location closer to home.

Before you choose a location for scattering the ashes of a family member or friend, give some thought to how you may feel later on. For example, if you choose to scatter the ashes in your own backyard, ask yourself how you will feel if you decide to sell the house and move away.

Other scatter locations prompt similar questions, including that of how other people might react. One example might be a public tennis court—a spot that might seem appropriate to family or friends, but one that other people might find offensive. Except in California, there are few if any restrictions on scattering properly pulverized ashes, so these are not so much legal questions as they are matters of taste, consideration for other people, and respect for the deceased.

Death seems to give us no choices, but it leaves our survivors with plenty of them. As Thomas Mann observed in *The Magic Mountain:* "A man's dying is more the survivor's affair than his own." Nowhere is this more true than in making or carrying out decisions about the disposition of a body after death.

Chapter **8**

What Price Is Right?

Let's face it. Unless your family has made other arrangements—by donating the body for scientific research or by planning ahead for direct burial or cremation—the death of a loved
one will bring you into contact with a profession no one really
wants to do business with.

That's not so much a criticism of funeral directors as a
comment on human nature. No matter how well they do their
job or how poorly, no matter how inexpensive or exorbitant the
price they charge, one thing is certain—none of their customers will go away eager to do business with them again. But since
nothing is more inevitable than death—and since relatively few
Americans take the "do it yourself" approach to preparing a
body for final disposition—most of us face fairly high chances
of doing business, or even repeat business, with a funeral
director.

Few lines of work inspire more grim humor and more bad
puns. Few businesses have received more biting criticism. And
yet few jobs have roots as deep in human history as the work of
caring for the dead.

Are funeral directors primarily business people with their
eye on the bottom line? Or are they professionals trained to
provide an important service in a time of need? Any look at the
modern American funeral industry can find evidence to support
either argument. The truth, of course, is that most successful
funeral directors are both.

No one is more aware of the contrasting ways in which their
work is viewed than funeral directors themselves. And, in some
cases, the funeral industry has helped to perpetuate the tensions
between those contrasting views.

Consider these comments, part of a summary of one of the
earliest conventions of the National Funeral Directors Association, which appeared in an 1885 issue of *Sunnyside*, a professional journal for the funeral industry:

"Funeral directors are members of an exalted, almost sacred calling . . . the Executive Committee believed that a cut in prices would be suicidal, and notified the manufacturers that better goods, rather than lower prices, were needed. . . . A $1,000 prize was offered for the best appearing corpse after 60 days . . . A resolution was passed requesting the newspapers in reporting the proceedings to refrain from flippancy."

Jessica Mitford cited those comments in her 1963 expose, *The American Way of Death*, a book which certainly failed to follow the profession's request to "refrain from flippancy."

Despite Ms. Mitford's barbs and other attempts to reform the rites and rituals with which Americans bury their dead, the overwhelming majority of American families still turn to the establishment that has become associated with the American way of death: a traditional funeral home featuring a range of caskets; embalming and restoration of the corpse (providing for the family what is sometimes described in the industry as a "beautiful memory picture" of the deceased); well-appointed viewing rooms; and, often, a chapel where the funeral service can be held.

Funeral directors describe their role as ushering grieving families through one of the most trying experiences life presents. They say they help families make the choices that will be most appropriate for their needs—that is, the arrangements that will be constructive in assuaging their grief, in helping them accept the death, and get on with the mourning period that follows.

For those reasons, funeral directors see themselves as trained professionals who, unlike salesmen for cemetery plots or burial vaults, must meet specific requirements to be licensed by the state.

Who's right? Are funerals too expensive? It all depends—on your own attitudes, the importance you attach to the expectations of your family and friends, and, ultimately, on your satisfaction with your dealings with a funeral home when a death occurs.

Whatever your feelings about the cost of dying, you are more likely to get the kind of treatment you want if you know what to expect. If you plan ahead, you will have more control over the bottom line—and that can be important. A death in the family can rank as a major expense.

Funeral costs vary widely. According to the National Funeral Directors Association, funeral costs for a typical adult can range from $2,500 to more than $8,000, with most falling between $2,700 and $5,500. For shorthand purposes, Robert Harden, the NFDA's executive director, uses a figure of $3,000 as the average cost of an American funeral. With two million deaths a year in the United States, the funeral industry is roughly a $6 billion a year business.

The single most expensive item in funeral costs is the casket. Mark-ups vary from funeral home to funeral home, but here are some general prices:

A majestic three-inch thick, hand-polished mahogany casket with the finest velvet interior can cost $12,000. Medium-priced wooden caskets, made of hardwood or oak, cost much less— probably between $1,200 and $4,000.

Metal caskets, such as steel, bronze or copper, generally cost more than the medium-priced wooden caskets. NFDA gives a range of $2,500 to $5,000 for a copper casket.

People who prefer a simple burial can choose a cloth-covered wooden casket or even a plain particle-board box, which can range in price from a couple of hundred dollars up to about $700. Corrugated-fiber boxes, often used for cremation, can be obtained from some funeral directors or crematories for prices ranging between $10 and $125.

Funeral establishments also charge for professional services, such as transferring the body to the funeral home, planning and organizing the funeral or memorial service, embalming, the use of a viewing room and a chapel, and the use of a hearse. But compared to the cost of a casket, most of these fees are relatively small. For instance, the NFDA gives the cost of embalming as $100 to $300.

Rather than simply denouncing the cost of dying, some critics focus on the lack of price competition in the industry. Lee Norrgard of the consumer affairs section of the American Association of Retired Persons notes that the primary goal of the FTC's Funeral Rule, strongly supported by AARP, was to encourage more competition. That has been only partially successful, at least in terms of reducing prices for consumers. In most parts of the country, funeral prices have remained basically the same, adjusted for inflation. There are exceptions, however. In Phoenix, Arizona, at least four funeral homes offer a traditional funeral for $1,500—half the cost of funerals in many other parts of the country.

The Federal Trade Commission requires that funeral establishments provide itemized price lists before purchase of services—either in person or on the telephone. Many funeral homes offer "packages," but you are not required to pay for items you have not used.

However, there's a catch here. Since there is no standardized price list and the price of specific services varies so much, it can be difficult to compare costs at different funeral homes. For instance, one funeral home may charge a $300 embalming fee, but provide a viewing room for free. Another may charge $150 for each item. Rather than focusing on the price of specific items or services, pay attention to the bottom line.

"Funeral costs" do not necessarily include other death-related expenses, such as the cost of a cemetery plot, a vault to line the grave (required by some cemeteries in order to keep the ground from sinking), and a fee for opening and closing the grave. These items can add up to a lot of money, usually about $2,000.

The cost of cemetery plots varies widely, depending on the cemetery and the region of the country. Before buying a plot, you should check prices at two cemeteries—preferably more.

And, like caskets, grave liners or vaults range in price according to the kind of material used, from a few hundred dollars to a couple of thousand. More expensive liners are often advertised as providing long-term protection for the body. It's true that a good vault or grave liner can protect the casket from such things as water seepage. But it can't stop the natural decay process that occurs even in an embalmed body.

The cost of opening and closing a grave varies widely, with the minimum usually at least $200 to $300, ranging upward to well over $1,000.

Cemeteries are not covered by the Federal Trade Commission's Funeral Rule, and are not bound by the requirements to give itemized price information either in person or by telephone. However, that is not often a problem—cemeteries often conduct extensive sales campaigns by telephone.

If you prefer a traditional earth burial, it can be a good idea to buy a cemetery plot beforehand. But beware of pressure to buy a vault, grave liner, or marker from the cemetery. Some cemeteries require liners or vaults and may also require a flat grave marker (making maintenance easier), but most states have laws against requiring people to purchase these goods from the cemetery. However, the laws don't always help a great deal, since cemeteries sometimes charge handling fees for goods purchased elsewhere and only a few states limit the size of these fees.

Since funeral directors can also sell vaults and grave liners, if you already have a cemetery plot when a death occurs, check with the cemetery's office to find out whether these items are actually required. Some funeral directors lead customers to believe they are required by the cemetery when that is not the case.

Alternatives

There are alternatives to the major expense of a traditional funeral. One is an "immediate burial," an interment without a formal viewing or embalming. The cost is usually kept low by making use of a simple container, a plain pinewood box, or perhaps one made of particle board or hard cardboard. These containers are much cheaper than traditional caskets, ranging in price from as little as $25 up to about $1,000.

Many funeral homes provide a package price for immediate burials and cremation. In both cases the average price is below $1,000. The price includes the container, transporting the body, care of the body for a day or perhaps more, and a fee for the funeral director's services.

In both cases, families can view the body privately and usually hold memorial services after the body has been buried or cremated.

Another way to cut funeral costs—and to make planning easier—is to join a memorial society in your area. These volunteer groups gather information on prices and arrangements, and some groups are able to contract with local funeral directors for special package rates for members. For information about memorial societies and a list of groups in your area, write to the Continental Association of Funeral and Memorial Societies (CAFMS), 2001 S Street N.W., Suite 630, Washington, D.C. 20009, or call (202) 462-8888. In Canada, contact Memorial Society Association of Canada, Box 96, Station A, Weston, Ontario M9N 3M6.

With proper planning, it is possible to forgo the services of a funeral director, which makes the disposition of the body even less expensive. For people interested in this alternative, I recommend two books: Ernest Morgan's "Dealing Creatively with Death: A Manual of Death Education and Simple Burial," available for $9.00 from Celo Press, Burnsville, N.C. 28714, and "Caring for Your Own Dead," by Lisa Carlson, $12.95, from Upper Access Publishers, Hinesburg, Vt. 05461.

The least expensive way of handling a body—but also perhaps the most worthwhile—is to donate it to a nearby medical school. It is best to contact the school beforehand and obtain a bequeathal form, although the decision to accept the body will be made at the time of death. Bequeathals can be made after a formal viewing and funeral, if the funeral director follows the school's directions for embalming. Many medical schools will also agree to return the ashes to the family.

Planning Ahead

Underlying much of the criticism of the funeral industry is the belief that in order to be dignified, the rituals of death should not be expensive or showy. In fact, many of Ms. Mitford's most ardent supporters are those whose sense of decorum would dictate a simple funeral with a minimum of fuss or expense. That is a value judgment—one that many Americans would agree with.

But not everyone is in accord—as the resilience of the American funeral industry illustrates. Even when they know simpler, less expensive alternatives are available, many families prefer to follow the practices accepted by their families and friends as "traditional."

Even so, there are plenty of instances where families have a far more elaborate funeral than they want or can afford. Given our reluctance to talk about death, that's not surprising. Unless families have taken the time to think through what they want in a funeral and what they think an appropriate tribute would be, they will probably be subject to assumptions or pressures, however subtle, for goods and services more elaborate or expensive than they would otherwise choose. Those pressures may come from funeral directors, but just as often they can come from family members or friends.

Taking time to plan ahead for the rites and rituals that are important to you and your family is the best way to avoid the emotional pressures that are almost inevitable in a time of grief.

Money is an important consideration in planning a funeral. But there are other things to take into account as well. One of them is finding a funeral director you trust, one with whom you will feel comfortable during an emotional and trying time.

If you do not know a funeral director in your area, here's some advice. Get together with a family member or friend—that makes the project less scary. Then call some local funeral homes and ask for an appointment. You might want to ask friends or acquaintances who have lived in the area for suggestions. Funeral directors should be happy to show you their public facilities and give you preliminary information about funeral expenses. However, don't expect an appointment on a walk-in basis.

The funeral business is one of the last bastions of the small American business, passed along from generation to generation, often with strong ties to a particular community or ethnic group. Just as it surely has its "bad apples"—every business does—it also has plenty of men and women who have learned through practice how to help people through the death of a loved one.

Ed Weber, a second-generation Baltimore funeral director, takes his role as a grief counselor seriously. "The real tragedy of the death of a loved one is when no one gains by it, when no one learns anything from it," he says. "Some funeral directors don't allow themselves to be touched by this process. That has to change."

There are many funeral directors who feel equally strongly about the meaningful role they play in helping a family come to terms with a death. As in any relationship, business or otherwise, there will be some funeral directors you feel more comfortable with than others. Meeting some face to face is a good way to help you decide which person you prefer to deal with.

If it is not possible for you to visit funeral homes, you can call them instead. They should be willing to give you information by telephone, as required by the Federal Trade Commission's Funeral Rule.

Prearranged Payments

A cautionary note: planning ahead does not necessarily mean paying ahead.

In recent years, along with encouraging people to come in for "pre-need arrangements," the funeral industry has also been encouraging "pre-pay" plans. In some cases, that may be an appropriate investment.

But these arrangements can also have drawbacks. Some

plans may not be transferable if you decide to move to be near a child or grandchild.

What if you change your mind about your arrangements? Not all plans can be altered.

It's also possible that pre-paying will tie your money up in an account earning less interest than the market rate.

Before signing up for a pre-paid funeral arrangement, do some checking on the plan you want to invest in. Call or write your local Better Business Bureau, consumer protection office, state insurance commissioner, attorney general or the funeral board to inquire about any complaints that may have been filed against the agent, the company, or the funeral home.

(A helpful report on various pre-pay plans is available from the American Association of Retired Persons. For one free copy of this report, as well as one on other funeral costs, write to AARP Fulfillment, 1909 K Street N.W., Washington, D.C. 20049. Ask for Product Reports: Prepaying Your Funeral? and Funeral Goods and Services.)

Protection for Consumers: The Funeral Rule

"O death, where is thy sting? O grave, where is thy victory? Where, indeed. Many a badly stung survivor, faced with the aftermath of some relative's funeral, has ruefully concluded that the victory has been won hands-down by a funeral establishment in disastrously unequal battle."

Those words launched Jessica Mitford's landmark attack on the American funeral industry in *The American Way of Death*. But the book's sensational effect was muted somewhat by the assassination of President John F. Kennedy soon after the book's publication. Even so, Mitford's criticisms were not forgotten. In 1964, Sen. Phillip Hart convened congressional hearings on the funeral industry.

The hearings caught the attention of the Federal Trade Commission, which eventually decided to consider consumer protection regulations for the funeral industry. But it was not until 1984 that the FTC's "funeral rule" actually went into effect and only after a court challenge from the funeral industry.

Here are the major provisions of the rule:

—The rule requires funeral establishments to make prices available to customers in person or over the phone early in the planning process. If price is a consideration, customers can then make the choices that best suit their budget.

—Funeral establishments cannot require customers to buy a complete funeral package, but must allow them to pick the items or services they actually need or want.

—Funeral establishments cannot require the purchase of a finished casket for a body that is to be cremated, although they can, if they choose, require an unfinished wooden box or alternate container.

—Funeral providers are required to make a good-faith effort to obtain permission prior to embalming a body.

—The rule also addresses a number of areas in which, in the FTC's judgment, some funeral providers may attempt to misrepresent the facts to customers. Examples would be false promises that embalming can preserve a body indefinitely or that a vault or grave liner will protect a body if that protection cannot be guaranteed. Funeral directors are also required to be truthful about legal provisions governing burial or cremation.

There is still some industry opposition to the funeral rule. But the opposition is far from solid. Many funeral directors now say that giving consumers assurance that they have some protection at a time when they are especially vulnerable protects the funeral industry as well as the customer. When people know funeral directors are treating them fairly, the funeral profession makes itself less vulnerable to the kind of attack Jessica Mitford made a quarter of a century ago.

Relatively few complaints result from the dispositions of the bodies of the 2 million Americans who die each year, whether the disposition is by means of a traditional funeral and burial, cremation, or donation of the body to science. According to Carol Jennings, the FTC's Funeral Rule coordinator, about four hundred complaints of violations were filed in the first five years after the Funeral Rule took effect. In that period, the FTC issued civil penalties in eleven cases.

Complaints about funerals can be filed at any number of places—consumer protection offices, Better Business Bureaus, or with the FTC itself. Violations of the Funeral Rule, however, should be reported directly to the FTC, Ms. Jennings says. (Write to: Federal Trade Commission, Pennsylvania Avenue and 6th Street N.W., Washington D.C. 20580, attention: Carol Jennings, Funeral Rule Coordinator).

You can also contact two consumer groups that were active in the FTC hearings reviewing the rule in 1988 and 1989. They are:

Continental Association of Funeral and Memorial Societies, 2001 S St. N.W., Suite 630, Washington, D.C. 20009.

A.A.R.P., 1909 K St. N.W., Washington, D.C. 20049, attention: Consumer Affairs.

Chapter 9

Rites and Rituals

There are people who almost make a hobby of attending funerals. There are others who'll do just about anything to avoid one.

Whatever our feelings about the traditional ceremonies that mark a death, for most of us there comes a time when we have to attend a funeral or memorial service. And, sooner or later, the sad time comes for most of us when we have to help plan one as well.

This chapter is designed for people in both groups.

What should you expect? What should you wear? What's the difference between a funeral and a memorial service? If you are mourning a friend or acquaintance, what else should you do in addition to attending the service itself? If you are responsible for helping to plan the service, what do you need to keep in mind?

Let's begin with an important distinction. The word "funeral" denotes a service at which the remains of the deceased are actually present. A memorial service is a ceremony without the body. Every funeral is a memorial service, but not every memorial service is a funeral.

Customs following death vary from region to region, and ethnic or religious groups often have their own distinctive practices. Yet there are almost always some common denominators.

In general, a death will be marked by a period of visitation when friends and relatives have a chance to see the family, express their condolences, and share their grief. In many cases, but not all, this includes a viewing of the body.

The visitation, which may last only a few hours or as long as three or four days, is usually the best attended part of the public activities that follow a death. The hours are more flexible and the occasion is less structured and formal than a service.

If the funeral or memorial service is being held at a time when you cannot attend, the visitation period gives you a chance to express condolences to the family. On the other hand, if you cannot get to the visitaton, your attendance at the service will mean a great deal.

Services vary in length and style, depending on the preferences of the family and the practices that are common in the community where they live. Religious services and rites usually follow a prescribed order, but that doesn't mean that families and clergy cannot personalize the ritual. Even highly formal rituals can include favorite hymns or scriptures of the deceased, or remarks that reflect the personality, accomplishments, or commitment of the life being remembered and celebrated.

A funeral is generally followed by another service, usually quite brief—the committal of the body to its final resting place. For instance, a church funeral may be followed by a procession to the cemetery and a brief graveside service.

Cremation can also be followed by a committal of the ashes to a niche in a columbarium, a structure with compartments designed for urns or other containers holding cremated remains. However, this ceremony is not necessarily held directly after the funeral or memorial service.

The final event is often a gathering of the family and close friends over a meal or refreshments. Sometimes the family expands this occasion; an example would be a reception to which all mourners at the service would be invited.

As for dress, there was a time when black, or at least a dark, somber color, was considered mandatory for such occasions. That's changing, and the time when family members were expected to wear black for an extended period is long gone. In many places, people are wearing bright, colorful clothes to funerals and memorial services. As a general rule, you should wear something you feel would be appropriate for a religious service.

The services themselves are also taking on new characteristics. Many religious services now focus more on celebrating the life that was lived than on bemoaning the fact that it has ended.

Another important change is that more clergy of all faiths

are making efforts to include participation by family and friends in the service, whether by reciting prayers, reading scripture, leading music, or delivering a eulogy. One of the first and most visible instances of such participation was the eulogy given by Senator Edward M. Kennedy at the funeral of his brother, Senator Robert F. Kennedy, in 1968.

"Funerals are a rite of passage, just as a wedding is," says Howard C. Raether, who was executive director of the National Funeral Directors Association for thirty-six years. Many people are writing their own wedding vows; the same kind of thing is happening in funeral and memorial services. Families and friends often want to create their own tributes to their loved ones, or at least add a personal touch to the ceremony.

"Post-death activities," to use the funeral industry's term, vary mainly in the length of the visitation period and in when the funeral is held. For instance, families on the East Coast may hold a visitation or wake for three or four nights, while a viewing on the West Coast is more likely to be restricted to a brief period just prior to the funeral or memorial service.

Mr. Raether has observed that evening services are becoming more common, since that time fits more easily into the work schedules of people who might want to come.

There is one characteristic of death observances that has remained remarkably the same: the importance of food. Friends and relatives still invariably shower the family of the deceased with good things to eat. In America, as in most cultures, the sharing of food becomes a symbol, subconscious or not, that paying respect to the dead should always include a concern for nourishing the living.

Why Have a Service?

Q: "I have been concerned for some time about whether a funeral—memorial service, graveside, whatever—is for the living or the dead, and about who should dictate the form, style, or size of such ceremonies.

"My grandfather is quite old, and in discussing his wishes with my mother and me (his only relatives), he said he wants family only, with a stark few words said over his grave—nothing more.

"He is widely known and respected and has a large number of friends all over the country, of all ages. They surely would be disappointed at not being allowed to pay their respects. And Mother and I feel that we would like to have some sort of ceremony to honor Grandpa and express our gratitude and love for him. However, he is a man of simple tastes and is vehement about not wanting fuss.

"In discussing our desires for last rites, my husband and I have come to feel that funeral ceremonies are held for the living, to help them cope with the loss of a loved one, and should be whatever the bereaved feel is helpful and appropriate.

"What is the best way to handle this question? We do not wish to show disregard or disrespect for the wishes of a departed loved one, but since he would be dead, couldn't we choose how to mark his departure?"—S.E.M., Eldersburg, Maryland

A: From earliest history, human beings have marked the deaths of their loved ones with ceremonies and other rituals. Often, there are religious reasons for certain practices—to ease the soul's entry into another world, for example.

But whether it is the stated reason or not, providing comfort to the living is always an important factor in the rituals surrounding death. Death is mysterious, awesome, and just plain scary.

When we lose a loved one, we need the strength and comfort that comes from gathering other people around us. We also feel the need to pay tribute to a life that was important to us, and to express our gratitude for that person's contributions to our own lives.

That is reason enough for you to want to mark your grandfather's death with some kind of ceremony. But "ceremony" doesn't have to mean "fuss."

There are a number of ways to satisfy your own needs that may even fit your grandfather's notions of decorum. Perhaps your grandfather is offended by the flowers, fancy caskets, limousines, and other accompaniments of many American funerals. But those are frills, not essentials, and it should be possible for you to find a funeral director or clergyperson who will help you arrange a simple ceremony.

Your grandfather indicated that he prefers a simple graveside service with only the family present. One possibility would be to hold a brief ceremony for the family at burial, then schedule a memorial service for a later time. Since your grandfather has friends in far-flung places, this may be more convenient for people who would want to come.

You're right. Death ceremonies are for the living. That is not to say that they should be planned in flagrant disregard of the wishes of the deceased. But in this case, I think you can in good conscience find a balance between your grandfather's desire for simplicity and lack of fuss and your own need to pay tribute to his life.

Making Rituals Meaningful

The rituals of death are meant to bring comfort to the bereaved. They should provide a way for mourners to express their grief and thus to begin the process of healing. These occasions give more comfort and take on more meaning when there is an attempt to make the service reflect the person whose life is being remembered.

This can be done in many ways—perhaps by including a

hymn, song, poem, or reading that was important to the person, or by having friends or family offer remarks or prayers.

A woman describes a personalized ceremony that she found especially meaningful:

"This past summer a member of our car club died. He was a music enthusiast and wanted a jazzy memorial. Another lady member and I led the service. It was done in good taste, and convinced a lot of people that we do not have to be conformists.

"We played a tape of some of his favorites, had a few poems and a message on love. It *was* Don. We are glad we did it.

"Now I truly believe I'm not asking too much of our children to have the same for us, on down the road, as I have been wishing. I already have most of the music and poems selected."
—D.H., Marshalltown, Iowa

Planning Personal Services

Whether they are religious or not, traditional or not, services after a death are important to survivors. They help us acknowledge that death is real, but they also provide a public way of remembering and paying tribute to the life that is now ended. Both of those purposes are important.

When Kim Gilpin's grandmother died in 1979, she felt she had lost not just a close and well-loved relative, but also an irreplaceable friend. She wanted to do something to honor Thelma Holthause as the family gathered to lay her body to rest.

She got her wish. Kim, then twenty-one, and her older cousin, Terry Holthause, joined their younger male cousins as pallbearers, carrying their grandmother's coffin into the church for the funeral service, back to the hearse, then to the gravesite at the cemetery.

In 1979 female pallbearers were unusual. Today, however, in some parts of the country, women are frequently asked to help bear the coffin of a friend or loved one.

"We felt it was something special we could do for Grandma," Kim Gilpin recalls. "It was nice that we were part of the family, a nice feeling to know that we were bearing our grandmother. I know she loved it."

Participating in her grandmother's funeral was special for another reason as well. When their grandfather died, Kim and her cousins were small children. She remembers that they were relegated to the very last car in the procession to the cemetery. And she remembers griping about that to her parents.

Her complaints apparently had an effect. J.E. Lowell Lemmon, Kim's father, was a second-generation funeral director and he believed strongly that participation in the funeral process is important for all survivors, including children. Mr. Lemmon, now deceased himself, encouraged survivors to consider all their family members, male as well as female, when they selected pallbearers. Grandchildren in their teens and twenties are often ideal candidates. But even younger children can be included by expanding the usual number of pallbearers from six to eight and by placing a strong, experienced bearer next to them.

A casket can weigh from 300 to 400 pounds. With six pallbearers an equal distribution of the weight would mean that each person must carry from 50 to 60 pounds, a load that many young people can handle with ease. In fact, however, some pallbearers invariably carry more weight than others, depending on where they are placed. A funeral director can easily place women, children, or inexperienced pallbearers in a spot where they can participate with confidence.

Funerals are not so much for the dead as for the living. Planning the ceremony, choosing a coffin, deciding who will carry it—all these details become part of a ritual that gives shape to days of grief as survivors come to terms with the fact of death.

Survivors, whether men or women, boys or girls, relatives or friends, need to be included in these activities. Grief is easier to bear when we feel that we can do something for someone we loved.

The details of a funeral can seem trivial in the face of the overwhelming fact of death. But it is details that keep us in touch with the truth that life goes on, that while we live we still face decisions and choices. Details can make the difference in any ceremony, and they can form the basis of fond memories just as they can plant the seeds of resentment.

Even now, years after her grandmother's death, Kim Gilpin is glad that she took an active role in the funeral. And even now, she remembers some details very clearly and offers a suggestion to future female pallbearers:

"Don't wear high heels," she cautions. "At the cemetery I remember sinking into the grass!"

Rituals are empty only if we allow them to be. Letting family members and friends participate—in big ways and small—is a good way to ensure that the services will contribute to the healing process that all mourners need.

Chapter 10

Cutting the Red Tape

It's endlessly fascinating to speculate about life after death. Unfortunately, when a death occurs, survivors are usually too busy with red tape to have much time to think about such things.

This chapter is designed to help survivors through some of the chores, legal and otherwise, that death brings on.

With a Little Help from Friends

When a death occurs, relatives and friends usually gather around the immediate family, bringing condolences and offers of help. Families do need help in these circumstances and here are ways to let other people take some of the burdens away:

—Ask someone to keep a list of phone calls and visitors and to keep track of telegrams, cards, letters, food, flowers, or other remembrances.

—You may also want someone else to answer the phone and the door. Visitors can be asked to sign a guest book. If you are having a viewing at a funeral home, a guest book will probably be provided there. But you will also want to know who visited you at home in order to acknowledge their kindness later.

—As family and friends gather, it will help if you have someone coordinating meals or other eating arrangements. Friends may bring in food, and someone should be available to organize the kitchen and help with serving and cleaning.

—If children will be present, arrange for infant care and for someone to watch toddlers. Consider asking older children in the family to help with younger children. Don't try to keep children out of sight. They need to feel included in the mourning process. After all, they have lost a loved one, too.

—If family members are coming from out of town, someone

may need to coordinate transportation to and from airports, train or bus stations. You may also need help arranging overnight accommodations.

—Make a list of friends, colleagues, or distant relatives who should be told about the death and informed about arrangements for a funeral or memorial service. Friends can help in notifying these people.

All too often, a natural reaction to the death of someone close to us is to withdraw, to pull away from other people. But this is the time when we most need the support of family and friends. The help they can offer in practical matters can help us through the first days of numbness and grief, when so many details need to be taken care of. Beyond the practical reasons, it is good therapy to let other people help out in a time of death or crisis. No matter how disinterested we may feel in other people, we will need them when, eventually, the numbness wears off and the time comes to rebuild a life without someone we loved.

There's another reason as well. The loss is not ours alone. Friends and relatives are grieving too. Helping out with details can be therapeutic for them, too. Death is a scary experience. But one of the good things that can come from it is the important reminder that the living can draw strength and support from one another.

Obituaries

Newspapers announce deaths in two ways, obituaries and death notices. Death notices are brief announcements, similar to classified ads, for which newspapers usually charge a fee. Funeral directors often write and place death notices as part of their services, but you can also do it yourself by calling the newspaper or delivering the information in person. The information included may vary from place to place, but in general you should furnish the full name, age, cause of death, place of birth, educational degrees, occupation, military service, membership in organizations, and a list of survivors in the immediate family.

Newspapers run obituaries as well. These are longer than death notices. They are considered news stories and are free of charge. In addition to the factual information included in a death notice, obituaries often emphasize contributions to a community or neighborhood, hobbies or interests, as well as any notable achievements or distinctions in the person's life. To find out how you can submit one call the newsroom of your newspaper and ask for the obituary desk. Guidelines vary from place to place, but many papers limit these stories only by the amount of space available.

Some newspapers recognize the value of obituaries as a way of recording the history and character of a community or city— and sharp editors recognize that obituaries draw a high readership. In recent years, some groups like the American Society of Newspaper Editors have given overdue recognition to obituary writers by giving awards for outstanding obituaries. That's an encouraging sign that newspapers may be paying more attention to an important service they can render their community.

Good obituaries should be just as interesting to read as a good news or feature story. Jim Nicholson of the *Philadelphia Daily News*, who won the 1987 ASNE award for obituary writing, included the following paragraphs in his March, 1986, obituary of Edward E. "Ace" Clark, an ice and coal dealer who hauled ice by horse-drawn wagon and truck for nearly forty years:

"His favorite among his horses . . . was one named Major. He could go into a house with ice, through the back door, across the alley and out the front door of the house in the next street, and Major, who knew the route, would walk himself around the block and be there waiting on the next street.

"'We used to say that if us kids had've been horses, we'd have been the best-raised kids in the neighborhood, because Dad knew more about horses than he did kids,' said his son, Bob Clark, with a laugh."

If you are providing information to a newspaper for an obituary, don't be afraid to convey the details or quirks—even humorous ones—that made a person special.

Taking Care of Business

Meanwhile, there will be plenty of other things keeping you busy. Here is a list of some of them:

—If you wish to have a religious service, contact a clergyperson. Discuss the type of service you want and ways they can make it more meaningful to you. Be aware, however, that ministers, priests, or rabbis conduct services within their own religious traditions, and many of them reserve the right to decline to include elements that may contradict their beliefs. For instance, some churches insist that every casket be covered by a plain pall rather than flowers or a flag, signifying the theological belief that every person is equal in death.

—If you plan to have a traditional funeral, you will need to select and notify pallbearers. In choosing them, don't overlook young people and women.

—If you don't want flowers, choose an appropriate recipient for any memorial contributions. If you do receive flowers, consider donating extra arrangements to a hospital or nursing home after the ceremony.

—You may want to arrange for someone to watch the house during the funeral or memorial service. When dates and times of services are printed in newspapers, thieves sometimes assume no one will be home and the house could be easy prey for a robbery.

—Notify your lawyer and the executor of the estate.

—Make arrangements to get copies of the death certificate. (See section below.)

—Locate important papers. If the estate is not in order, keep every piece of mail that comes in for at least the first three months. Routine notices and announcements can be clues of stocks, bonds, mutual fund ownership, debts, or other obligations that survivors may have no knowledge of.

—Notify the person's employer and arrange to check on benefits available to survivors of employees.

—Call the person's insurance agent or life insurance company. Check for all life insurance policies, casualty and death benefits.

—If the person was a veteran, contact the nearest office of the Department of Veterans Affairs to inquire about benefits (See section below.)

—Contact the local Social Security office to check your eligibility for a lump-sum death benefit and to inquire about applying for monthly benefits.

—Survivors of civil service workers may be eligible for benefits from the Civil Service Bureau of Retirement, Insurance and Occupational Health (1900 E Street N.W., Washington, D.C. 20415.)

—Notify organizations of which the person was a member.

This list is not exhaustive. After a death, survivors of even the best organized person face a long trail of paperwork. The person who has died is freed from worldly cares. But survivors are left with a maze of red tape. All too often, they are ill-equipped to face it.

Twenty years ago, the Life Insurance Marketing and Research Association (LIMRA) undertook a study of widows and found that most of them did not have the financial information that was essential to settling an estate and arranging their own future.

"What Do You Do Now?" is the seventy-eight-page guidebook that grew out of that study. Now in its twenty-fifth printing, the booklet has expanded its focus beyond widows to include all beneficiaries.

Its contents serve as a handy checklist of things that should be done, from the first calls that must be made after a death, whether anticipated or unexpected, to sections on handling grief and arranging for organs to be donated.

The booklet is available to the public through many local life insurance agents. LIMRA member companies and their representatives may obtain the booklet for $2 per copy, with discounts available for quantity orders. Nonmembers of LIMRA can obtain the booklet for 50 percent more. To order, call 800–235–4672 (203–677–0033 for Connecticut residents and those outside the contiguous United States). Or write to LIMRA, P.O. Box 208, Hartford, Connecticut 06141.

Death Certificates and Government Benefits

Q: "Where are death certificates obtained, and how many does one need? I know they are needed for insurance purposes, but that is all I know. Is there a charge for them?

"What about Social Security and veterans benefits? How does one go about securing the forms?"—J.B., San Diego

A: The death certificate is the official legal document you will need in order to settle an estate or establish claims for benefits. It is issued by the office of vital statistics in your city or town. There is usually a small charge, but the amount varies from state to state.

You will need several copies of the certificate, but photocopies are not sufficient. The raised registrar's seal is essential in order to make the certificate a valid legal document, which means you must pay the fee for each one.

The number of copies you need will depend on the complexity of the estate you are settling. Some deaths will require only one or two; others may need more than a dozen.

As a general rule, it is probably a good idea to get at least ten or twelve, although one financial adviser I spoke with says he advises clients to estimate how many they will need, then add ten. "You may find a need for one years later," he says.

You will need a death certificate to settle each of your insurance policies, as well as for claiming benefits from an employer, transferring ownership of stocks and bonds, cars, houses, etc. In general, you will need a separate certificate for each transaction.

Obtaining a death certificate is not difficult, but you probably will need to show identification in order to prove your need for the certificate. Be ready for the red tape and the waiting-in-line that is part of dealing with a bureaucracy. That can make the task inconvenient, especially at a time when you are still grieving the death.

Most funeral directors will offer to obtain death certificates for you, and this service is sometimes included in the general service fee, although some funeral directors may list it as a separate charge.

If the service is already included in your fees, you should be charged only for the actual costs incurred in obtaining the certificates: the cost of the certificates themselves and perhaps a courier fee.

If the deceased was covered by Social Security, most funeral directors will contact the local Social Security office to notify them of the death. But you will still need to make an appointment for yourself to apply for benefits. You can find the phone number listed under government offices and it's best to call as soon as possible. Benefits are not sent automatically and you need to get the paperwork started.

If the deceased was a veteran, you should also contact the nearest Veterans Administration office to determine funeral benefits. Your funeral director can also help you with this and should have the necessary forms on hand.

Where There's a Will There's a Way

Q: "What happens if I die without a will?"—J.T.L., Baltimore

A: A will enables you to decide what will happen to your property after you die. If you have left no instructions, or if your instructions do not meet the legal requirements for a will, then your estate will be settled according to state laws.

The legal term for dying without a will is dying "intestate," which comes from the Latin words *in*, meaning not, and *testatus*, having made a valid will or testament.

In practical terms, dying intestate means you're simply handing your business over to the government. Whatever you leave behind will be parceled out according to your state's formula, rather than your own preferences.

These formulas can get quite complicated. For instance, in Maryland, if a person dies intestate and leaves behind a spouse and children, state law decrees that the spouse shall get one-third of the estate, with the rest divided among the children. If the deceased has no children, but does leave a spouse as well as a surviving parent, the spouse gets one-half of the estate, with the rest going to the parent. Each state has its own formula.

In other words, if you are married and die without a will, your spouse will not automatically inherit your entire estate— except for property for which there is legal evidence that you have joint ownership, such as a deed to your house or a car registration on which you are listed as co-owner.

If you are single and have no children, your parents generally inherit the estate. (This provision can come as a nasty surprise to unmarried couples who live together and have no will.)

If your parents are dead, the search for possible heirs widens to your parents' children (your brothers and sisters or stepbrothers and stepsisters), grandparents, uncles or aunts, cousins, stepchildren or even godparents and their children. The rules governing who would be on the list and the order in which they would be considered may vary from state to state, as does the formula for parceling out the estate.

If no heirs are found, your estate will revert to the state under a legal concept known as "escheat."

Each state designates a use for this money. In Maryland, for example, such property is converted into cash, and the proceeds are given to the school board of the county in which the deceased lived.

Even if the formula your state follows for such cases sounds fair for your situation, you should keep in mind that dying intestate greatly increases the chances that your survivors will tie up your estate in court, possibly eating away its value with legal fees.

If you have no heirs, you might prefer to decide who will get your property, rather than having it auctioned off on behalf of the local school board.

Your estate belongs to you—but only until you die. A will gives you the assurance that at your death your property will be distributed according to your wishes, not the wishes of the state.

Veterans' Benefits

Q: "I'm a veteran, and from time to time I've thought I might like to be buried in Arlington Cemetery. How do I go about finding out if that's possible?"—C.P., Georgia

A: Arlington Cemetery, located just across the Potomac River from Washington, D.C., is the nation's best-known military cemetery. Because space for traditional casket burial is limited, the Department of the Army, which supervises the cemetery, has placed restrictions on eligibility for interment at Arlington.

A member of any branch of the U.S. armed services who dies while on active duty can be buried at Arlington. Veterans who have been honorably discharged are eligible if they have received any one of the following awards: Purple Heart, Silver Star, Distinguished Service Medal, Distinguished Service Cross, Air Force Cross, Navy Cross, or the Medal of Honor.

In addition, any veteran who was honorably discharged prior to October 1, 1949, and who was given a physical disability rating of 30 percent or greater at the time of separation, is also eligible for ground burial. Spouses of eligible veterans who do not remarry can be buried in the same gravesite.

Arlington Cemetery also has a columbarium, an open-air courtyard consisting of above-ground concrete walls with niches for urns containing cremated remains. This facility is open to any veteran whose last period of service ended with an honorable discharge. The niches are sealed with a marble marker and are designed to hold two urns, to allow for future "inurnment" of spouses.

Plots in Arlington are not preassigned and arrangements for burial there cannot be made prior to the veteran's death. But, according to officials at the cemetery, it is possible to clear up any questions about eligibility beforehand by writing to the Superintendent, Arlington National Cemetery, Arlington, Va. 22211.

If you or a member of your family is eligible for casket burial at Arlington, here is the procedure to follow:

Upon the veteran's death, you or your funeral director should contact Arlington officials by calling (202) 695–3250 or 695–3255, any day except Sunday. The family will need to provide information about the veteran's service record in order to verify eligibility.

If you do not have a copy of the discharge papers, the following information will be sufficient: Serial number, date of entry into service, date of discharge, and rank at the time of discharge. Burials at Arlington take place five days a week.

Families who desire to place a veteran's remains in the columbarium can contact the cemetery directly, or, if they prefer, their funeral director can make the arrangements.

Even if you are not eligible for burial at Arlington, there are death benefits that you and your family should be aware of.

The Department of Veterans Affairs operates 111 national cemeteries located throughout the country, 65 of which still have available burial space. These cemeteries are open to all veterans of active duty who left the military with any discharge other than dishonorable.

Veterans of the Reserve and the National Guard who die

while performing, or as a result of performing, active duty for training are also eligible. Some of these cemeteries also have a columbarium for cremated remains.

Burial in a national cemetery includes a standard grave marker, and families are given a flag for the casket. Spouses and dependent children can be buried in the same gravesite, and they are eligible for burial even if they die before the veteran.

Veterans who do not choose to be buried in a national cemetery are still eligible for a flag and a standard government grave marker or memorial plaque, or for an equivalent amount of money that can be applied to a privately purchased marker. The reimbursement rate for grave markers is around seventy dollars.

Veterans who have a service-connected disability are eligible for additional funds for funeral and burial expenses.

It is not possible to choose a gravesite beforehand. But it is helpful to family members if a veteran has made his or her burial wishes known. At the time of death, the family can then make appropriate burial arrangements through a funeral director.

According to Department of Veterans Affairs officials, most funeral directors are familiar with the procedures and may even provide the necessary forms. However, it is always helpful for the family to have information about the veteran's service record readily available.

Department of Veterans Affairs regional offices in your city or state can answer further questions about your eligibility for death and burial benefits. You can find the number in the white pages of your telephone directory. In many directories toll-free numbers are also listed under "U.S. Government."

In addition to national cemeteries, several states operate their own system of veterans cemeteries. Department of Veterans Affairs offices can tell you whether your state has such a program and where the nearest state and national cemeteries are located.

Epilogue

A week after an earthquake in Armenia killed as many as 25,000 people in December, 1988, a survivor tried to describe the emotional paralysis that gripped the survivors who were faced with such overwhelming devastation.

Here, through a translator, is the gist of what he said: "When people die here, neighbors and friends gather with the family to weep. If someone doesn't cry, we say they have a heart of stone. But now, with so much death around us, everyone has a heart of stone."

No wonder. In the face of such a cataclysmic disaster, the grief most people feel after a death becomes an emotional luxury. How could their grief ever end? Which relative or friend would they grieve for first or most? How could one person's grief ever be adequate to the loss of whole families or entire cities?

Staying alive through such a tragedy is only the first step of survival. As Armenians began the task of rebuilding their towns and villages, they also began the harder process of healing their emotional and spiritual wounds, of finding the faith and hope on which to build not just new houses, but new lives.

In the face of death, human beings can show amazing resilience. Over and over, we see hope rising where rational observers would think the human spirit had been crushed as thoroughly as the buildings of those Armenian towns. Times like that remind us that hope for the future is itself a victory over disaster and death.

Yet in the aftermath of disaster hope comes hard. The same can be true after the death of someone we love.

Psychologists who study the aftermath of disasters warn that survivors encounter problems in the years ahead. They often search for people to blame—and probably find some. Some are tormented with questions and guilt, wondering why they

115

survived when others did not. Many are tempted to drown their pain with alcohol or drugs.

Those kinds of problems will sound familiar to many grieving people. That's why it helps to remember that survival is more than a one-time stroke of luck or fate; it is also a long, complicated, up-and-down process. Survivors sometimes carry their scars for a lifetime.

But history shows us that, despite our scars, we humans can overcome even overwhelming disasters. Experience also tells us that we can survive the personal disasters that don't make headlines, the deaths of family members and friends that scar our own lives.

Even when the world seems to come to an end, as in Armenia, those who survive in the long run learn to affirm life again. It's not quick or easy, but true survivors will find their way back to life. When they do, they will find that, with time, the stones inside them will again become hearts, able to accept love and give it in return.